Lecture Notes
in Business Information Processing   119

Series Editors

Wil van der Aalst
Eindhoven Technical University, The Netherlands
John Mylopoulos
University of Trento, Italy
Michael Rosemann
Queensland University of Technology, Brisbane, Qld, Australia
Michael J. Shaw
University of Illinois, Urbana-Champaign, IL, USA
Clemens Szyperski
Microsoft Research, Redmond, WA, USA

T0218389

Esther David   Valentin Robu
Onn Shehory   Sebastian Stein
Andreas Symeonidis (Eds.)

Agent-Mediated Electronic Commerce

Designing Trading Strategies and Mechanisms for Electronic Markets

AMEC 2011, Taipei, Taiwan, May 2, 2011
and TADA 2011, Barcelona, Spain, July 17, 2011
Revised Selected Papers

 Springer

Volume Editors

Esther David
Ashkelon Academic College
Ashkelon, Israel
E-mail: astrdod@acad.ash-college.ac.il

Valentin Robu
University of Southampton
Southampton, UK
E-mail: vr2@ecs.soton.ac.uk

Onn Shehory
IBM Haifa Research Lab
Haifa, Israel
E-mail: onn@il.ibm.com

Sebastian Stein
University of Southampton
Southampton, UK
E-mail: ss2@ecs.soton.ac.uk

Andreas Symeonidis
Aristotle University of Thessaloniki
Thessaloniki, Greece
E-mail: asymeon@eng.auth.gr

ISSN 1865-1348   e-ISSN 1865-1356
ISBN 978-3-642-34888-4   e-ISBN 978-3-642-34889-1
DOI 10.1007/978-3-642-34889-1
Springer Heidelberg Dordrecht London New York

Library of Congress Control Number: 2012951308

ACM Computing Classification (1998): K.4.4, J.1, I.2.11, H.3.5

Typesetting: Camera-ready by author, data conversion by Scientific Publishing Services, Chennai, India

Printed on acid-free paper

Springer is part of Springer Science+Business Media (www.springer.com)

Preface

Recent years have witnessed a vast increase in the number, diversity, and complexity of electronic marketplaces. Such distributed electronic markets are frequently seen as an essential tool for efficient allocation of resources in a variety of fields, ranging from electronic commerce, financial markets, distributed supply chain management, to next-generation power grids or the allocation of user attention space in online advertising. The rapid growth in these areas has also led to increasing interest into developing tools for the efficient automation of market-based interactions. In some areas, such automation is already a reality. For example, most of the trading occurring in financial markets is performed by algorithmic strategies, and much of the advertising space on the Web is allocated by automated engines.

Multi-agent systems, which consist of autonomous, proactive, and interacting software components, have long been identified as an important solution for the efficient automation of electronic markets. Unlike humans, automated trading agents are able to react almost instantaneously to changes in the market and perform exponentially more transactions in a matter of seconds. However, efficient automation of large-scale markets using multi-agent techniques requires addressing a host of complex challenges. Perhaps the most easily recognized challenge in designing and using such a system is the lack of centralized control. Agents are autonomous actors that take their own decisions, rather than simply deterministically executing operations assigned to them by their owners. Another important challenge in multi-agent systems is the presence of uncertainty, i.e., incomplete or imperfect information, both regarding the market environment, the preferences, strategies and behavior of the other agents and, sometimes, even uncertainty in specifying the agent's own preferences. Furthermore, agents are boundedly rational actors and often have to make decisions in limited time, under risk aversion, or based on other constraints imposed by their owners or the market environment. In order to deal which these challenges, the science underpinning multi-agent systems draws from a variety of diverse disciplines ranging from artificial intelligence, operations research, and machine learning to economics and game theory.

These trends are also evidenced by the papers collected in this volume, which are revised and extended versions of work that appeared at two leading international workshops on electronic markets held in 2011. The first is the 13th International Workshop on Agent Mediated Electronic Commerce (AMEC 2011), co-located with the 10th International Conference on Autonomous Agents and Multiagent Systems (AAMAS 2011) conference in Taipei, Taiwan, and the second is the International Workshop on Trading Agent Design and Analysis (TADA 2011), co-located with the 22nd International Joint Conference on Artificial Intelligence (IJCAI 2011) in Barcelona, Spain.

The papers presented at these workshops illustrate both the depth and the broad range of research topics in this field. They range from providing solutions to open theoretical problems in online scheduling and bargaining under uncertainty, to designing bidding agents in a wide range of application areas, such as electronic commerce, supply chain management, or keyword advertising, to designing agents that can successfully replicate actual human behaviors in realistic games.

In a theoretical line of work, Ceppi et al. consider the problem of designing equilibrium strategies for non-cooperative bargaining with arbitrary one-sided uncertainty. They provide an algorithm to solve bargaining with any type of one-sided uncertainty, and show its computational complexity is polynomial with two types, while with more types the problem becomes hard. Wu et al. consider the problem of designing efficient acceptance strategies for agents in online scheduling, and compare the performance of online solutions to the theoretically optimal offline strategies.

Taking a human-agent interaction perspective, Kim et al. address the challenge of evaluating the fidelity of autonomous agents that are attempting to replicate human behaviors. The authors introduce and investigate the Social Ultimatum Game and discuss the efficacy of a set of metrics in comparing various autonomous agents to human behavior collected from experiments. Rosenfeld et al. study the domain of recommender systems, and describe the algorithms used in a hybrid recommender and the authors' experience in designing a pilot application in recommending alternative products in an online shopping environment.

A number of papers discuss novel strategies developed for different tracks of the Trading Agent Competition (TAC). Chatzidimitriou et al., Siranovic et al., and Tsung et al. propose strategies for trading agents participating in the TAC Ad Auctions game. Groves and Gini propose a method for improving predictions in the Supply Chain Management (SCM) game, by integrating multivariate and temporal aspects of partial least squares (PLS) regression. Rayner et al. discuss the testing of expectation models in continuous double auctions against empirical facts, while Tsekourakis and Symeonidis propose a method for dealing with trust and reputation in unreliable multi-agent trading environments.

Overall, we hope the papers in this volume will offer readers a comprehensive and informative snapshot of the current state of the art in this stimulating and timely area of research.

Finally, we would like to thank the members of the Program Committees of both workshops for careful reviews, which significantly improved the presentation of the papers and helped ensure the high quality of the papers included in these proceedings. We are also grateful to all of the authors for submitting their papers, and for their efforts in carefully revising their papers for this volume. Finally, we would like to thank the participants to both workshops for their questions and lively discussions, which contributed greatly to the success of these events.

August 2012

Esther David
Valentin Robu
Onn Shehory
Sebastian Stein
Andreas Symeonidis

Organization

AMEC Workshop Organizers

Esther David   Ashkelon Academic College, Israel
Valentin Robu   University of Southampton, UK
Onn Shehory   IBM Haifa Research Lab, Israel
Sebastian Stein   University of Southampton, UK

TADA Workshop Organizer

Andreas Symeonidis   Aristotle University of Thessaloniki, Greece

Program Committee

Bo An   University of Massachusetts, Amherst, USA
Michael Benisch   Carnegie Mellon University, USA
Ken Brown   University College Cork, Ireland
Maria Chli   Aston University, UK
John Collins   University of Minnesota, USA
Florin Constantin   Georgia Institute of Technology, USA
Yagil Engel   IBM Research, Haifa, Israel
Maria Fasli   Essex University, UK
Shaheen Fatima   Loughborough University, UK
Nicola Gatti   Politecnico di Milano, Italy
Enrico Gerding   University of Southampton, UK
Maria Gini   University of Minnesota, USA
Amy Greenwald   Brown University, USA
Mingyu Guo   University of Liverpool, UK
Noam Hazon   Carnegie Mellon University, USA
Minghua He   Aston University, UK
Sverker Janson   SICS, Sweden
Patrick Jordan   University of Michigan, USA
Radu Jurca   Google, Switzerland
Wolfgang Ketter   Erasmus University, The Netherlands
Han La Poutré   CWI, The Netherlands
Jérôme Lang   Université Paris-Dauphine, France
Kate Larson   University of Waterloo, Canada
Kevin Leyton-Brown   University of British Columbia, Canada
Peter McBurney   King's College London, UK
Pericles A. Mitkas   Aristotle University of Thessaloniki, Greece
Tracy Mullen   Penn State University, USA

Table of Contents

Non–cooperative Bargaining with Arbitrary One–Sided Uncertainty

Sofia Ceppi, Nicola Gatti, and Claudio Iuliano

Dipartimento di Elettronica e Informazione, Politecnico di Milano
Piazza Leonardo da Vinci 32, I-20133 Milano, Italy
{ceppi,ngatti,iuliano}@elet.polimi.it

Abstract. Non-cooperative bargaining is modeled as an extensive–form game with uncertain information and infinite actions. Its resolution is a long–standing open problem and no algorithm addressing uncertainty over multiple parameters is known. We provide an algorithm to solve bargaining with any kind of one–sided uncertainty. Our algorithm reduces a bargaining problem to a finite game, solves this last game, and then maps its strategies with the original continuous game. Computational complexity is polynomial with two types, while with more types the problem is hard and only small settings can be solved in exact way.

1 Introduction

The automation of economic transactions through negotiating software agents is receiving a large attention in the artificial intelligence community. Autonomous agents can lead to economic contracts more efficient than those drawn up by humans, saving also time and resources [14]. We focus on the main bilateral negotiation setting: the *bilateral bargaining*. This setting is characterized by the interaction of two agents, a *buyer* and a *seller*, who can cooperate to produce a utility surplus by reaching an economic agreement, but they are in conflict on what specific agreement to reach. The most expressive model for non–cooperative bargaining is the *alternating–offers* [11]: agents alternately act in turns and each agent can accept the offer made by her opponent at the previous turn or make a new offer. Agents' utility over the agreements depends on some parameters: *discount factor*, *deadline*, *reservation price*. In real–world settings, agents have a Bayesian prior over the values of the opponents' parameters.

The alternating–offers is an *infinite–horizon* (agents can indefinitely bargain) *extensive–form* (the game is sequential) *Bayesian* (information is uncertain) game and the number of available actions to each agent is infinite (an offer is a real value). The appropriate solution concept is the *sequential equilibrium* [8]. The game theoretic study of bargaining with uncertain information is an open challenging problem. No work presented in the literature so far is applicable regardless of the uncertainty *kind* (i.e., the uncertain parameters) and *degree* (i.e., the number of the parameters' possible values). Microeconomics provides analytical results for settings without deadlines, for single uncertainty kinds,

E. David et al. (Eds.): AMEC/TADA 2011, LNBIP 119, pp. 1–14, 2013.

and with narrow degrees of uncertainty, e.g., over the discount factor of one agent with two possible values [12] and over the reservation price of both agents with two possible values per agent [1]. Computer science provides algorithms to search for sequential equilibria [9] only with finite games and without producing belief systems off the equilibrium path. This makes such algorithms not suitable for bargaining. Several efforts have been accomplished to extend the backward induction algorithm to solve games with uncertain information [4]. However, as shown in [5], the solutions produced by these algorithms may not be equilibria. Finally, the algorithm provided by [5] solves settings with one–sided uncertain deadlines, but its extension to general settings appears to be impractical due to the mathematical machinery it needs.

The work in [5] provides the unique known computational complexity result, showing that with one–sided uncertain deadlines the problem is polynomial in the length of the bargaining independently of the number of types. However, this uncertainty situation is very special because all the types have the same utility functions before their deadlines. This fact leads all the types whose deadline is not expired to have the same behavior, drastically reducing thus the complexity of the problem. When discount factors and reservation prices are uncertain, the types have different utility functions and we expect that they have different optimal behaviors. The difficulty of developing an exact algorithm for the bargaining problem pushed the scientific community to produce approximate solutions. A large number of tactic–based heuristics are available, e.g., see [3], but none provides bounds over the solution quality in terms of ϵ–Nash equilibrium.

In this paper, after having reviewed the alternating–offers protocol and its solution with complete information (Section 2), and after having discussed the model with uncertainty (Section 3), we present a sound and complete algorithm to solve settings with arbitrary kinds and degrees of uncertainty (Section 4). Our algorithm reduces the bargaining game to a finite game, solves this last game, and finally maps its equilibirum strategies to the original continuous game. We initially focus on settings with two possible types. We define a belief system $\overline{\mu}$ and a strategy profile $\overline{\sigma}$ where agents can make a finite number of offers and the randomization probabilities with which agents make such offers are parameters. To compute the values of these parameters such that $(\overline{\mu}, \overline{\sigma})$ is a sequential equilibrium, we build a finite game and we provide an algorithm based on support–enumeration to solve it. We show that the problem is polynomial in the deadline length. Then, we extend the algorithm to more than two types by exploiting mathematical programming and we experimentally evaluate it.

2 Bargaining Model and Complete Information Solution

We present the alternating–offers protocol [11] with deadlines. There are two agents, a buyer **b** and a seller **s**, who can play alternatively at discrete time points $t \in \mathbb{N}$. The function $\iota : \mathbb{N} \to \{\mathbf{b}, \mathbf{s}\}$ returns the agent that plays at time point t, and it is such that $\iota(t) \neq \iota(t+1)$. We study single–issue bargaining because our aim is the study of settings with uncertainty and algorithms for single–issue problems can be easily extended to multi–issue problems as it is shown in [4,2]. Agents bargain on the value of a variable $x \in \mathbb{R}$, e.g., representing the price. The pure strategies $\sigma_{\iota(t)}(t)$ available to agent $\iota(t)$ at $t > 0$ are: $offer(x)$, where x is the offer for the issue; $accept$, that concludes the bargaining with an agreement, formally denoted by (x,t), where x is such that $\sigma_{\iota(t-1)}(t-1) = offer(x)$ (i.e., the value offered at $t-1$), and t is the time point at which the offer is accepted; $exit$, that concludes the bargaining with a disagreement, formally denoted by $NoAgreement$. At $t = 0$ only actions $offer(x)$ and $exit$ are available.

Seller's and buyer's utility functions, denoted by $U_s : (\mathbb{R} \times \mathbb{N}) \cup NoAgreement \to \mathbb{R}$ and $U_b : (\mathbb{R} \times \mathbb{N}) \cup NoAgreement \to \mathbb{R}$ respectively, return the agents' utility for each possible outcome. Each utility function depends on the following parameters: the reservation prices, denoted by $RP_b \in \mathbb{R}^+$ and $RP_s \in \mathbb{R}^+$ for buyer and seller respectively (we assume $RP_b \geq RP_s$), the discount factor, denoted by $\delta_b \in (0,1]$ and $\delta_s \in (0,1]$ for buyer and seller respectively, and the deadlines, denoted by $T_b \in \mathbb{N}$ and $T_s \in \mathbb{N}$ for buyer and seller respectively. The buyer's utility function is:

$$U_b(\cdot) = \begin{cases} NoAgreement & 0 \\ (x,t) & \begin{cases} (RP_b - x) \cdot (\delta_b)^t & \text{if } t \leq T_b \\ \epsilon & \text{otherwise} \end{cases} \end{cases},$$

where $\epsilon < 0$ (after T_i, $U_i(x,t)$ is strictly negative and thus agent i strictly prefers to leave the game rather than reaching any agreement). The seller's utility function is analogous, except for $U_s(x,t) = (x - RP_s) \cdot (\delta_s)^t$ if $t \leq T_s$.

With complete information, the appropriate solution concept is the *subgame perfect equilibrium*. The solution can be found by using backward induction as follows. We call $T = \min\{T_b, T_s\}$ and we call $x^*(t)$ the $\iota(t)$'s best offer at t, if this offer exists. It can be easily observed that the outcome of each subgame which starts at $t \geq T$ is $NoAgreement$, because at least one agent strictly prefers to exit the game rather than to reach any agreement. Now we consider the subgame which starts at $t = T - 1$. This subgame is essentially an *ultimatum game* [6]. $\iota(T)$ accepts any offer x such that $U_{\iota(T)}(x,T) \geq 0$ ($x \leq RP_b$ if $\iota(T) = b$ and $x \geq RP_s$ if $\iota(T) = s$), she leaves the game otherwise. The $\iota(T-1)$'s optimal offer $x^*(T-1)$ maximizes $\iota(T-1)$'s utility (i.e., $x^*(T-1) = RP_b$ if $\iota(T-1) = s$ and $x^*(T-1) = RP_s$ if $\iota(T-1) = b$). The subgames which start at time $t < T-1$ can be studied in a similar way. Suppose that we have found $x^*(t+1)$ and that we want to derive $x^*(t)$. We can consider the subgame composed of time points t and $t+1$ as an ultimatum game variation in which $\iota(t+1)$ accepts any offer x such that $U_{\iota(t+1)}(x,t+1) \geq U_{\iota(t+1)}(x^*(t+1),t+2)$ and offers $x^*(t+1)$ otherwise. The $\iota(t)$'s best offer, among all the acceptable offers at time point $t+1$, is the one which maximizes $\iota(t)$'s utility. We can compute this offer as:

$$x^*(t) = \begin{cases} RP_s + (x^*(t+1) - RP_s) \cdot \delta_s & \text{if } \iota(t) = b \\ RP_b - (RP_b - x^*(t+1)) \cdot \delta_b & \text{if } \iota(t) = s \end{cases}.$$

The computation of the values $x^*(t)$ is linear in t. We report the buyer's subgame perfect equilibrium strategies (the seller's ones are analogous):

$$
\sigma_{\mathbf{b}}^*(t) = \begin{cases} t = 0 & \textit{offer}(x^*(0)) \\ 0 < t < T & \begin{cases} \textit{accept} & \text{if s's offer} \leq x^*(t-1) \\ \textit{offer}(x^*(t)) & \text{otherwise} \end{cases} \\ t = T & \begin{cases} \textit{accept} & \text{if s's offer} \leq x^*(t-1) \\ \textit{exit} & \text{otherwise} \end{cases} \\ t > T & \textit{exit} \end{cases}
$$

3   Introducing Uncertainty

We consider one–sided uncertain settings where the buyer's parameters are uncertain to the seller (the reverse situation is analogous). Our game is an imperfect–information game in which the buyer can be of different types, each one with different values of $RP_{\mathbf{b}}$, $\delta_{\mathbf{b}}$, and $T_{\mathbf{b}}$. Uncertainty is over the actual type of the buyer. For the sake of presentation, we describe our algorithm for the basic case where the number of buyer's types is two, we call them $\mathbf{b_1}$ and $\mathbf{b_2}$. Then, we discuss how to extend it with more than two types. Without loss of generality we assume $T_{\mathbf{b_1}} \leq T_{\mathbf{b_2}}$. We call $\mu(t) = \langle \Theta_{\mathbf{b}}(t), P_{\mathbf{b}}(t) \rangle$ the s's beliefs about b's type where $\Theta_{\mathbf{b}}(t) \in \wp(\{\mathbf{b_1}, \mathbf{b_2}\})/\varnothing$ and $P_{\mathbf{b}}(t) = \{\omega_{\mathbf{b_1}}(t), \omega_{\mathbf{b_2}}(t)\}$ ($\wp$ denotes the power set and $\omega_{\mathbf{b_i}}(t)$ denotes the probability that b's type is $\mathbf{b_i}$ at time t). $\mu(0)$ are data of the problem.

Example 31. *The parameters values are:* $RP_s = 0$, $\delta_s = 0.75$, $T_s = 10$; $RP_{\mathbf{b_1}} = 1$, $\delta_{\mathbf{b_1}} = 0.7$, $T_{\mathbf{b_1}} = 5$; *the* $\mathbf{b_2}$ *'s parameters values are:* $RP_{\mathbf{b_2}} = 0.9$, $\delta_{\mathbf{b_2}} = 0.8$, $T_{\mathbf{b_2}} = 5$. *Assume that* $\iota(0) = \mathbf{b}$ *and that the values* $\omega_{\mathbf{b_1}}(0)$ *and* $\omega_{\mathbf{b_2}}(0)$ *are arbitrary.*

The appropriate solution concept is the sequential equilibrium [8]. It is a couple $a = (\mu, \sigma)$, also called assessment, in which μ is a belief system that specifies how agents must update their beliefs during the game and σ is the agents' strategy profile that specifies how they must act. μ must be *consistent* with σ and σ must be *sequentially rational* given μ. On the equilibrium path, μ is consistent to σ if it is equal to the beliefs derived from σ by using the Bayes rule. Off the equilibrium path, the Bayes rule is not applicable and two notions of consistency can be employed: *weak consistency* does not pose any constraint, while *strong consistency* requires that a sequence of fully mixed strategies exists such that its limit converges to σ and that the limit of the sequence of beliefs derived from the fully mixed strategies by using the Bayes rule converges to μ. In bargaining problems, strong consistency is commonly used because it allows one to exclude non reasonable equilibria. We remark that every game admits at least one strong sequential equilibrium. Off the equilibrium path we impose that is, if at time point t we have $\omega_{\mathbf{b_i}}(t) = 0$, then for any $\tau > t$ we keep $\omega_{\mathbf{b_i}}(\tau) = 0$.

4   The Algorithm

Since bargaining with uncertainty may not admit any equilibrium in pure strategies, as shown in [5], we directly search for equilibria in mixed strategies. The basic idea behind our work is to solve the bargaining problem by reducing it to a finite game, deriving equilibrium strategies such that on the equilibrium path the agents can act only a finite set of actions, and then by searching for the agents' optimal strategies on the path. Our work is structured in the following three steps. 1) We analytically derive an assessment $\bar{a} = (\bar{\mu}, \bar{\sigma})$ in which the randomization probabilities of the agents are parameters and such that, when the parameters' values satisfy some conditions, $\bar{a}$ is a sequential equilibrium. 2) We formulate the problem of finding the values of the agents' randomization probabilities in $\bar{a}$ as the problem of finding a sequential equilibrium in a reduced bargaining game with finite actions, and we prove that there always exist values such that $\bar{a}$ is a sequential equilibrium. 3) We develop an algorithm based on support enumeration to solve the reduced game when the types are two and we show that its computational complexity is polynomial in the agents' deadlines. Then we develop an algorithm based on linear complementarity mathematical programming to solve the case with more than two types.

4.1 Deriving Equilibrium Strategies

Without loss of generality, on the equilibrium path we study only time points $t < T_{\mathbf{b}_1}$. This is because, if agents reach time points $t \geq T_{\mathbf{b}_1}$ on the equilibrium path, then the bargaining at t is a game with complete-information in which agents are $\mathbf{b}_2$ and $\mathbf{s}$. Indeed, $\mathbf{b}_1$ never makes offers at time $t \geq T_{\mathbf{b}_1}$, action *exit* being the dominant action, and therefore, if action *offer(x)* is observed at $t \geq T_{\mathbf{b}_1}$, the Bayes rule imposes that $\omega_{\mathbf{b}_1}(t) = 0$. We build an assessment $\bar{a}$ such that, on the equilibrium path, the $\iota(t)$'s offers at $t < T_{\mathbf{b}_1}$ belong to a finite set $X(t) := \{x^*_{\mathbf{b}_i}(t) : \forall i\}$, where $x^*_{\mathbf{b}_i}(t)$ is the $\iota(t)$'s optimal offer at t in the corresponding complete-information game between $\mathbf{b}_i$ and $\mathbf{s}$ computed as previously discussed. Offering at t any $x \notin X(t)$ does not allow $\iota(t)$ to improve her expected utility. In Fig. 1 we show $x^*_{\mathbf{b}_1}(t)$ and $x^*_{\mathbf{b}_2}(t)$ related to Example 31. We connect the offers $x^*_{\mathbf{b}_1}(t)$ with a dotted line and the offers $x^*_{\mathbf{b}_2}(t)$ with a dashed line.

We focus on $\bar{a}$. For each $t < T_{\mathbf{b}_1}$ we rank the values in $X(t)$ in increasing order and we call $\mathbf{b}_w = \arg\max_{i \in \{\mathbf{b}_1, \mathbf{b}_2\}} \{x^*_i(0)\}$ and $\mathbf{b}_s = \arg\min_{i \in \{\mathbf{b}_1, \mathbf{b}_2\}} \{x^*_i(0)\}$ where w means *weak* and s means *strong*. In Fig. 1 we have $\mathbf{b}_w = \mathbf{b}_1$ and $\mathbf{b}_s = \mathbf{b}_2$. According to [13], the adjectives 'strong' and 'weak' refer to the contractual power

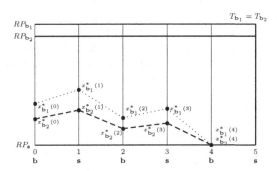

Fig. 1. $x^*_{\mathbf{b}_i}(t)$ in the complete information games between $\mathbf{s}$ and $\mathbf{b}_i$ (see Example 31)

of the corresponding buyer's type: in complete–information settings the seller's expected utility is larger when it bargains with $\mathbf{b}_w$ rather than when it bargains with $\mathbf{b}_s$. In two cases, the type with the strongest contractual power at $t = 0$ is not the strongest for all $t > 0$. This happens, first, when there exists at least a time point t where $x^*_{\mathbf{b}_s}(t) > x^*_{\mathbf{b}_w}(t)$, second, when $T_{\mathbf{b}_w} > T_{\mathbf{b}_s}$. These two cases represent two exceptions that can be easly tackled by modifying the computation of $x^*_{\mathbf{b}_s}(t)$ and $x^*_{\mathbf{b}_w}(t)$. For reasons of space, we omit their description. The basic idea behind $\bar{a}$ is that, when agents are forced to make the offers in $X(t)$, $\mathbf{b}_w$ can gain utility from disguising herself as $\mathbf{b}_s$, making the optimal $\mathbf{b}_s$'s offers, while $\mathbf{b}_s$ prefers to signal her own type, making offers different from the $\mathbf{b}_w$'s ones. That is, $\mathbf{b}_w$ acts in order to increase her expected utility with respect to the situation where $\mathbf{s}$ believes $\mathbf{b}$'s type to be $\mathbf{b}_w$ with certainty. The same idea is used in [1].

We focus on the buyer's behaviour. On the equilibrium path, $\mathbf{b}_w$ randomizes between offering $x^*_{\mathbf{b}_w}(t)$ (or, equivalently, accepting $x^*_{\mathbf{b}_w}(t-1)$) and offering $x^*_{\mathbf{b}_s}(t)$ (the offer $x^*_{\mathbf{b}_s}(t-1)$ is always accepted, leading to the largest possible utility), whereas $\mathbf{b}_s$ offers $x^*_{\mathbf{b}_s}(t)$ in pure strategies (or, equivalently, accepts $x^*_{\mathbf{b}_s}(t-1)$). We denote by $1-\alpha(t)$ and $\alpha(t)$ the $\mathbf{b}_w$'s randomization probabilities over offering $x^*_{\mathbf{b}_w}(t)$/accepting $x^*_{\mathbf{b}_w}(t-1)$ and offering $x^*_{\mathbf{b}_s}(t)$, respectively, and we consider $\alpha(t)$ as parameters. We remark that, if $\alpha(t) = 1$, then the strategies of $\mathbf{b}_w$ and $\mathbf{b}_s$ are pure and they are the same. On the equilibrium path, the beliefs are updated according to the Bayes rule. We call $\omega^*_{\mathbf{b}_i}(t)$ the probability over type $\mathbf{b}_i$ at time t produced according to the Bayes rule after that $\mathbf{b}$ made $\mathit{offer}(x^*_{\mathbf{b}_s}(t-1))$ at time $t-1$. We have $\omega^*_{\mathbf{b}_s}(t) = \frac{\omega_{\mathbf{b}_s}(t-1)}{\alpha(t-1)\omega_{\mathbf{b}_w}(t-1)+\omega_{\mathbf{b}_s}(t-1)}$ and $\omega^*_{\mathbf{b}_w}(t) = 1 - \omega^*_{\mathbf{b}_s}(t)$. We notice that when the strategies are pure, if $\alpha(t-1) = 1$, then $\omega^*_{\mathbf{b}_w}(t) = \omega_{\mathbf{b}_w}(t-1)$ and $\omega^*_{\mathbf{b}_s}(t) = \omega_{\mathbf{b}_s}(t-1)$, while, if $\alpha(t-1) = 0$, then $\omega^*_{\mathbf{b}_w}(t) = 0$ and $\omega^*_{\mathbf{b}_s}(t) = 1$.

To characterize $\mathbf{b}$'s strategies off the equilibrium path, at each time t we divide the domain of x as: $\mathcal{D}1 := (x^*_{\mathbf{b}_w}(t-1), +\infty)$, $\mathcal{D}2 := (x^*_{\mathbf{b}_s}(t-1), x^*_{\mathbf{b}_w}(t-1)]$, $\mathcal{D}3 := (-\infty, x^*_{\mathbf{b}_s}(t-1)]$. We call y the value such that $\sigma_{\mathbf{s}}(t-1) = \mathit{offer}(y)$. The $\mathbf{b}_w$'s strategies are: if $y \in \mathcal{D}1$, then y is rejected; if $y \in \mathcal{D}2$, then y is accepted with probability of $1-\alpha(t)$ and rejected to offer $x^*_{\mathbf{b}_s}$ otherwise, and, if $y \in \mathcal{D}3$, then the offer is accepted (no better agreement can be reached from time point $t+1$ on). The $\mathbf{b}_s$'s strategies are exactly her optimal strategies in the complete–information game between $\mathbf{b}_s$ and $\mathbf{s}$: if $y \in \mathcal{D}1$ or $y \in \mathcal{D}2$, then the offer is refused and, if $y \in \mathcal{D}3$, then the offer is accepted. We notice that, if $\alpha(t) = 1$, then $\mathbf{b}_w$ and $\mathbf{b}_s$ have the same strategies also off the equilibrium path. Formally, the strategies are (at $t > T_{\mathbf{b}_1}$ the buyer's strategies are those with complete information; the strategies in the case in which the buyer's type is $\mathbf{b}_s$ and $\omega_{\mathbf{b}_s}(t) = 0$ are):

$$
\sigma^*_{\mathbf{b}_w}(t) = \begin{cases} t=0 & \begin{cases} \mathit{offer}(x^*_{\mathbf{b}_w}(0)) & 1-\alpha(0) \\ \mathit{offer}(x^*_{\mathbf{b}_s}(0)) & \alpha(0) \end{cases} \\ 0 < t < T_{\mathbf{b}_1} & \begin{cases} y \in \mathcal{D}1 & \begin{cases} \mathit{offer}(x^*_{\mathbf{b}_w}(t)) & 1-\alpha(t) \\ \mathit{offer}(x^*_{\mathbf{b}_s}(t)) & \alpha(t) \end{cases} \\ y \in \mathcal{D}2 & \begin{cases} accept & 1-\alpha(t) \\ \mathit{offer}(x^*_{\mathbf{b}_s}(t)) & \alpha(t) \end{cases} \\ y \in \mathcal{D}3 & accept \end{cases} \end{cases}
$$

$$
\sigma^*_{\mathbf{b}_s}(t) = \begin{cases} t=0 & \mathit{offer}(x^*_{\mathbf{b}_s}(0)) \\ 0 < t < T_{\mathbf{b}_1} & \begin{cases} y \in \mathcal{D}1, \mathcal{D}2 & \mathit{offer}(x^*_{\mathbf{b}_s}(t)) \\ y \in \mathcal{D}3 & accept \end{cases} \end{cases}
$$

To characterize the beliefs and s's strategies off the equilibrium path, at each time t we divide the domain of x as: $\mathcal{D}1' := [x^*_{\mathbf{b}_w}(t-1), +\infty)$, $\mathcal{D}2' := [x^*_{\mathbf{b}_s}(t-1), x^*_{\mathbf{b}_w}(t-1))$, $\mathcal{D}3' := (-\infty, x^*_{\mathbf{b}_s}(t-1))$. We call y the value such that $\sigma_{\mathbf{b}}(t-1) = \mathit{offer}(y)$. If $\omega_{\mathbf{b}_w}(t-1) > 0$, then the beliefs are: if $y \in \mathcal{D}1'$, then $\mathbf{b}$ is believed $\mathbf{b}_w$ with a probability of 1; if $y \in \mathcal{D}3'$, then the probabilities of $\mathbf{b}$'s types are the same that we compute on the equilibrium path when $y = x^*_{\mathbf{b}_s}(t-1)$; if $y \in \mathcal{D}2'$, then the $\mathbf{b}_s$'s probability increases linearly in y such that, if y goes to $x^*_{\mathbf{b}_w}(t-1)$, then $\omega_{\mathbf{b}_s}(t)$ goes to 0 and, if y goes to $x^*_{\mathbf{b}_s}(t-1)$, then $\omega_{\mathbf{b}_s}(t)$ goes to $\omega^*_{\mathbf{b}_s}(t)$ (notice that we cannot use '=', since the cases with '=' are on the equilibrium path). Defining $\kappa(t,y) = \frac{x^*_{\mathbf{b}_w}(t)-y}{x^*_{\mathbf{b}_w}(t)-x^*_{\mathbf{b}_s}(t)}$, the belief system is:

$$\bar{\mu}(t) = \begin{cases} y \in \mathcal{D}1' & \omega_{\mathbf{b}_s}(t) = 0 \\ y \in \mathcal{D}2' & \omega_{\mathbf{b}_s}(t) = \omega^*_{\mathbf{b}_s}(t)\kappa(t-1,y) \\ y \in \mathcal{D}3' & \omega_{\mathbf{b}_s}(t) = \omega^*_{\mathbf{b}_s}(t) \end{cases}.$$

We focus on the seller's behaviour. On the equilibrium path, s randomizes between offering $x^*_{\mathbf{b}_s}(t)$ (or, equivalently, accepting $x^*_{\mathbf{b}_s}(t-1)$) and offering $x^*_{\mathbf{b}_w}(t)$ (the offer $x^*_{\mathbf{b}_w}(t-1)$ is always accepted, leading to the largest possible utility). We denote by $\beta(t)$ and $1-\beta(t)$ the s's randomization probabilities over offering $x^*_{\mathbf{b}_s}(t)$/accepting $x^*_{\mathbf{b}_s}(t-1)$ and offering $x^*_{\mathbf{b}_w}(t)$, respectively, and we consider $\beta(t)$ as parameters. Off the equilibrium path, the s's strategies are: if $y \in \mathcal{D}1'$, then the offer is accepted; if $y \in \mathcal{D}2'$, then the acceptance probability decreases linearly in y such that, if y goes to $x^*_{\mathbf{b}_w}(t-1)$, then it goes to 1 and, if y goes to $x^*_{\mathbf{b}_s}(t-1)$, then it goes to $\beta(t)$ (the s's probability to offer $x^*_{\mathbf{b}_w}(t)$ is 1 minus the acceptance probability); if $y \in \mathcal{D}3'$, then it is rejected to offer $x^*_{\mathbf{b}_w}(t)$ if $\beta(t) < 1$ and $x^*_{\mathbf{b}_s}(t)$ otherwise. Formally the strategies are (at $t > T_{\mathbf{b}_1}$ the seller's strategies are those with complete information):

$$\sigma^*_{\mathbf{s}}(t) = \begin{cases} t=0 & \begin{cases} \mathit{offer}(x^*_{\mathbf{b}_w}(0)) & 1-\beta(0) \\ \mathit{offer}(x^*_{\mathbf{b}_s}(0)) & \beta(0) \end{cases} \\ 0 < t < T_{\mathbf{b}_1} & \begin{cases} y \in \mathcal{D}1' & \mathit{accept} \\ y \in \mathcal{D}2' & \begin{cases} \mathit{offer}(x^*_{\mathbf{b}_w}(t)) & \kappa(t-1,y)(1-\beta(t)) \\ \mathit{accept} & 1-\kappa(t-1,y)(1-\beta(t)) \end{cases} \\ y \in \mathcal{D}3' & \begin{cases} \mathit{offer}(x^*_{\mathbf{b}_w}(t)) & \lceil 1-\beta(t)\rceil \\ \mathit{offer}(x^*_{\mathbf{b}_s}(t)) & \lfloor\beta(t)\rfloor \end{cases} \end{cases} \end{cases}.$$

Call $\bar{\sigma} = (\sigma^*_{\mathbf{b}_w}, \sigma^*_{\mathbf{b}_s}, \sigma^*_{\mathbf{s}})$. We state the following theorem.

Theorem 41. *If $\alpha(t), \beta(t) \in [0,1]$ are such that, limited to the offers in $X(t)$, $\bar{\sigma}$ is sequentially rational given $\bar{\mu}$, then $\bar{a} = (\bar{\mu}, \bar{\sigma})$ is a sequential equilibrium.*

Proof. We assume that there are values $\alpha(t), \beta(t) \in [0,1]$ such that, limited to the offers in $X(t)$, $\bar{\sigma}$ is sequentially rational given $\bar{\mu}$ and we prove: (i) sequential rationality off the equilibrium path and (ii) Kreps and Wilson's consistency. (The computation of the values of $\alpha(t), \beta(t)$ is discussed in the following sections.)

To prove (i) we need to show that agents cannot gain more by making offers not belonging to $X(t)$. At first, we characterize agents' strategies on the equilibrium path because it is useful for our proof. We do not consider the trivial cases in which $\omega_{\mathbf{b}_w}(0) = 1$ or $\omega_{\mathbf{b}_s}(0) = 1$; they can be solved as complete–information games. It can be easily observed that if $\omega_{\mathbf{b}_w}(0) < 1$ then $\alpha(t) > 0$ for every

t. Indeed, let suppose $\iota(0) = \mathbf{b}$ and $\omega_{\mathbf{b}_w}(0) < 1$, if $\alpha(0) = 0$, then $\mathbf{b}_w$ and $\mathbf{b}_s$ make different offers at time $t = 0$ and $\mathbf{s}$ accepts both of them at $t = 1$. In this case $\mathbf{b}_w$ can increase her utility acting as $\mathbf{b}_s$. Thus, two situations are possible: either $0 < \alpha(t) < 1$ or $\alpha(t) = 1$. If $0 < \alpha(t) < 1$, then $\mathbf{b}_w$ randomizes between offering $x_{\mathbf{b}_w}(t)$ and $x_{\mathbf{b}_s}(t)$, so necessarily $0 < \beta(t + 1) < 1$ because the game is non–degenerate. Otherwise, if $\alpha(t) = 1$, then necessarily $\beta(t+1) = 1$ because the game in non-degenerate and the case $\beta(t + 1) = 0$ cannot lead to an equilibrium ($\mathbf{b}_w$ can increase her utility by offering $x^*_{\mathbf{b}_w}(t)$ that will be always accepted).

Now, we are in the position to prove sequential rationality off the equilibrium path. We focus on the case $0 < \alpha(t) < 1$ and $0 < \beta(t + 1) < 1$. We consider $\mathbf{b}_w$. Offering any $x > x^*_{\mathbf{b}_w}(t)$ at time t is dominated by offering $x^*_{\mathbf{b}_w}(t)$ because all these offers are accepted with a probability of one and $x^*_{\mathbf{b}_w}(t)$ gives a larger utility to $\mathbf{b}_w$. By construction, all the offers $x^*_{\mathbf{b}_s}(t) < x < x^*_{\mathbf{b}_w}(t)$ give to $\mathbf{b}_w$ the same expected utility and all the offers $x < x^*_{\mathbf{b}_s}(t)$ are rejected, so the $\mathbf{b}_w$'s expected utility cannot be increased by performing them. In a similar way, it is possible to analyze the strategies of $\mathbf{b}_s$ and $\mathbf{s}$. In the case of $\mathbf{s}$, if she acts at $t = 0$ or $t > 0$ after that $\mathbf{b}$ makes an off–equilibrium–path offer, her strategy will be pure. It can be shown that, if $\sigma_{\mathbf{b}}(t - 1) = \mathit{offer}(x)$ with $x < x^*_{\mathbf{b}_s}(t - 1)$ and $\beta(t) < 1$, then $\mathbf{s}$'s optimal action is to offer $x^*_{\mathbf{b}_w}(t)$. Therefore, agents cannot gain more by making offers not belonging to $X(t)$.

In order to prove (ii), we need to provide a fully mixed strategy $\sigma_{\mathbf{b}_i,n}(t)$ such that $\lim_{n\to\infty} \sigma_{\mathbf{b}_i,n}(t) = \sigma^*_{\mathbf{b}_i}(t)$ and $\lim_{n\to\infty} \omega_{\mathbf{b}_i,n}(t) = \omega_{\mathbf{b}_i}(t)$ where $\omega_{\mathbf{b}_i,n}(t)$ are the sequences of beliefs derived from $\sigma_{\mathbf{b}_i,n}(t)$ by Bayes rule and $\omega_{\mathbf{b}_i}(t)$ are the beliefs prescribed by $\mu(t)$. The fully mixed strategies are:

$$
\sigma_{\mathbf{b}_w,n}(t) = \begin{cases} y > x^*_{\mathbf{b}_w}(t) & \frac{1}{n} \\ y = x^*_{\mathbf{b}_w}(t) & 1 - \alpha(t) - A(n) \\ x^*_{\mathbf{b}_w}(t) > y > \overline{y} & \frac{1}{n} \\ \overline{y} \geq y > x^*_{\mathbf{b}_s}(t) & 1 - (1-\alpha(t))\frac{y - x^*_{\mathbf{b}_s}(t)}{n(\overline{y}-x^*_{\mathbf{b}_s}(t))} \\ y = x^*_{\mathbf{b}_s}(t) & \alpha(t) - A(n) \\ x^*_{\mathbf{b}_s}(t) > y & \frac{\alpha(t)}{n} \end{cases}, \sigma_{\mathbf{b}_s,n}(t) = \begin{cases} y \geq x^*_{\mathbf{b}_w}(t) & \frac{1}{n^{\mathcal{T}_{b1}}} \\ x^*_{\mathbf{b}_w}(t) > y > \overline{y} & \frac{x^*_{\mathbf{b}_w}(t)-y}{n(x^*_{\mathbf{b}_w}(t)-\overline{y})} \\ \overline{y} \geq y > x^*_{\mathbf{b}_s}(t) & \frac{1}{n} \\ y = x^*_{\mathbf{b}_s}(t) & 1 - B(n) \\ x^*_{\mathbf{b}_s}(t) > y & \frac{1}{n} \end{cases},
$$

where $A(n)$ and $B(n)$ are functions of n such that they go to zero as n goes to infinity and the sum over the probabilities of all actions is one.   □

4.2   Building the Reduced Bargaining Game

The previous section drastically reduces the complexity of solving a bargaining game, leaving open only the determination of the values of the randomization probabilities such that Theorem 41 holds. In this section, we formulate the problem of computing these values as the problem of solving a reduced bargaining game with finite actions. Since each finite game admits at least one equilibrium strategy, there always exist values such that Theorem 41 holds.

To compute the values of $\alpha(t)$ and $\beta(t)$ we "extract" the equilibrium path prescribed by assessment $\bar{a}$ given in the previous section. We build an imperfect–information extensive–form game with finite actions. It can be represented by a game tree built as follows. Fig. 2 depicts the tree related to Example 31; for the sake of simplicity, we denote *accept* by 'A' and *offer(x)* by 'x'; A' and A'' label two different As of the same buyer's type at the same t. In the root of the tree, *nature* plays drawing the buyer's type: $\mathbf{b}_1$ or $\mathbf{b}_2$ with probability $\omega_{\mathbf{b}_1}(0)$ and $\omega_{\mathbf{b}_2}(0)$, respectively. Since the game is with imperfect information, s cannot distinguish whether her opponent's type is $\mathbf{b}_1$ or $\mathbf{b}_2$ unless she observes an action that can be made only by $\mathbf{b}_1$ or by $\mathbf{b}_2$, respectively (e.g., in Fig. 2, action $x^*_{\mathbf{b}_1}(0)$ can be accomplished only by $\mathbf{b}_1$). Customarily in game theory, decision nodes that an agent cannot distinguish constitute an *information set* (in Fig. 2, dashed lines connect decision nodes of the same information set).

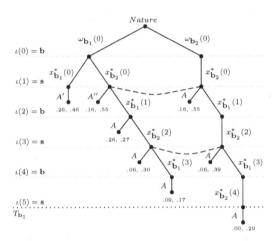

Fig. 2. Tree of the reduced game related to Example 31. We denote *accept* by A and *offer(x)* by value x. We report utilities $U_{\mathbf{s}}(x,t), U_{\mathbf{b}}(x,t)$ under the terminal nodes.

Let be $t = 0$. If $\iota(0) = \mathbf{b}$, the available actions are *offer(x)* with $x \in X(0)$ if $\mathbf{b}_i = \mathbf{b}_w$ and $x = x^*_{\mathbf{b}_s}(0)$ if $\mathbf{b}_i = \mathbf{b}_s$ (we recall that in Example 31, $\mathbf{b}_1 = \mathbf{b}_w$ and $\mathbf{b}_2 = \mathbf{b}_s$). When $\iota(0) = \mathbf{s}$, the available actions are *offer(x)* with $x \in X(0)$.

Let be $0 < t < T_{\mathbf{b}_1} - 1$. Suppose $\iota(t) = \mathbf{b}$. If $\mathbf{b}_i = \mathbf{b}_w$ and $\sigma_{\mathbf{s}}(t-1) = offer(x^*_{\mathbf{b}_s}(t-1))$, then the only possible action is *accept*, otherwise, if $\sigma_{\mathbf{s}}(t-1) = offer(x^*_{\mathbf{b}_w}(t-1))$, the available actions are *accept* and *offer($x^*_{\mathbf{b}_s}(t)$)*. Action *accept* at time t leads to a terminal node in which the agents reach the agreement (x,t) where x is such that $\sigma_{\iota(t-1)}(t-1) = offer(x)$. In Fig. 2, under the terminal nodes, we report the agents' utilities $U_{\mathbf{s}}(x,t), U_{\mathbf{b}}(x,t)$. If $\mathbf{b}_i = \mathbf{b}_s$ and $\sigma_{\mathbf{s}}(t-1) = offer(x^*_{\mathbf{b}_s}(t-1))$ then the only possible action is *accept*, otherwise, if $\sigma_{\mathbf{s}}(t-1) = offer(x^*_{\mathbf{b}_w}(t-1))$, the only available action is *offer($x^*_{\mathbf{b}_s}(t)$)*. Suppose $\iota(t) = \mathbf{s}$. If $\sigma_{\mathbf{b}}(t-1) = offer(x^*_{\mathbf{b}_s}(t-1))$ then the only possible action is *accept*, otherwise, if $\sigma_{\mathbf{b}}(t-1) = offer(x^*_{\mathbf{b}_s}(t-1))$, the available actions are *accept* and *offer($x^*_{\mathbf{b}_w}(t)$)*.

Let be $t = T_{\mathbf{b}_1} - 1$. If $x^*_{\mathbf{b}_w}(t) > x^*_{\mathbf{b}_s}(t)$, the tree building rules are those described for the previous case. Otherwise, if $x^*_{\mathbf{b}_w}(t) = x^*_{\mathbf{b}_s}(t)$, when $\mathbf{b}_i = \mathbf{b}_w$ and $\sigma_{\mathbf{s}}(t-1) = offer(x^*_{\mathbf{b}_w}(t))$ the only available action is *accept*, as in Example 31 (see Fig. 1).

There cannot be any equilibrium when a buyer's type $\mathbf{b}_i$ randomizes at t over accepting and offering offers of the same sequence of offers $x^*_{\mathbf{b}_i}(t)$.

We notice that the size of the tree is linear in $T_{\mathbf{b}_1}$. The values of $\alpha(t)$ and $\beta(t)$ can be computed finding a sequential equilibrium in the above reduced bargaining problem. By definition, the value of $\alpha(t)$ is equal to the probability with which $\mathbf{b}_w$ makes $offer(x^*_{\mathbf{b}_s}(t))$ at t in the reduced bargaining game, while the value of $1 - \beta(t)$ is equal to the probability with which $\mathbf{s}$ makes $offer(x^*_{\mathbf{b}_w}(t))$ at t in the reduced bargaining game. Since any finite game admits at least one sequential equilibrium, there always exist values of $\alpha(t)$ and $\beta(t)$ such that $\bar{a}$ is a strong sequential equilibrium, namely, Theorem 41 always holds.

4.3   Solving the Reduced Bargaining Game

To compute an equilibrium, at first we represent the game in the sequence form [7] where agents' actions are sequences in the game tree.

The sequence form is represented with a sparse matrix in which the agent i's actions are the sequences of her extensive form actions connecting the root of the tree to any information set of i. To avoid confusion, we shall use 'sequence' for the actions of the sequence form and 'action' for the actions of the extensive-form. For the sake of simplicity, we define different $\mathbf{b}$'s sequences for each different type. Considering the game tree reported in Fig. 2, the set of agent i's sequences Q_i is:
$Q_{\mathbf{s}} = \{\varnothing, \langle A' \rangle, \langle A'' \rangle, \langle x^*_{\mathbf{b}_1}(1) \rangle, \langle x^*_{\mathbf{b}_1}(1), A \rangle, \langle x^*_{\mathbf{b}_1}(1), x^*_{\mathbf{b}_1}(3) \rangle, \langle x^*_{\mathbf{b}_1}(1), x^*_{\mathbf{b}_1}(3), A \rangle\}$,
$Q_{\mathbf{b}_1} = \{\varnothing, \langle x^*_{\mathbf{b}_1}(0) \rangle, \langle x^*_{\mathbf{b}_2}(0) \rangle, \langle x^*_{\mathbf{b}_2}(0), A \rangle, \langle x^*_{\mathbf{b}_2}(0), x^*_{\mathbf{b}_2}(2) \rangle, \langle x^*_{\mathbf{b}_2}(0), x^*_{\mathbf{b}_2}(2), A \rangle\}$,
$Q_{\mathbf{b}_2} = \{\varnothing, \langle x^*_{\mathbf{b}_2}(0) \rangle, \langle x^*_{\mathbf{b}_2}(0), x^*_{\mathbf{b}_2}(2) \rangle, \langle x^*_{\mathbf{b}_2}(0), x^*_{\mathbf{b}_2}(2), x^*_{\mathbf{b}_2}(4) \rangle\}$; where $\varnothing$ is the empty sequence. Given two sequences q and q' with $q \in Q_{\mathbf{b}_i}$ and $q' \in Q_{\mathbf{s}}$, the payoffs are non–null only if the node reached performing the combination of sequences q and q' is a terminal node. Let consider the subtree of type $\mathbf{b}_1$ shown in Fig. 2. The node reached performing $q = \langle x^*_{\mathbf{b}_2}(0) \rangle$ and $q' = \langle x^*_{\mathbf{b}_1}(1) \rangle$ is a non terminal node and, therefore, the payoffs are null, whereas the node reached performing $q = \langle x^*_{\mathbf{b}_2}(0) \rangle$ and $q' = \langle A'' \rangle$ is a terminal node and the payoffs are $U_{\mathbf{s}} = 0.16$ and $U_{\mathbf{b}} = 0.55$. We show in Table 1 the payoff bimatrix for $\mathbf{b}_1$ and $\mathbf{s}$ (for reason of space we omit the empty sequences $\varnothing$). The payoff bimatrix for $\mathbf{b}_2$ and $\mathbf{s}$ is defined similarly.

The sequence form presents some constraints over the probabilities with which the sequences are played by agents. We denote by $p_i(q)$ the probability with which agent i makes sequence q. The constraints on the probabilities of the empty sequences are (by convention, we set $\omega_{\mathbf{s}}(0) = 1$):

Table 1. Payoff bimatrix for $\mathbf{b}_1$ and $\mathbf{s}$

$\mathbf{b}_1, \mathbf{s}$	A'	A''	$x^*_{\mathbf{b}_1}(1)$	$x^*_{\mathbf{b}_1}(1), A$	$x^*_{\mathbf{b}_1}(1), x^*_{\mathbf{b}_1}(3)$
$x^*_{\mathbf{b}_1}(0)$	.26, .46	–	–	–	–
$x^*_{\mathbf{b}_2}(0)$	–	.16, .55	–	–	–
$x^*_{\mathbf{b}_2}(0), A$	–	–	.26, .27	–	–
$x^*_{\mathbf{b}_2}(0), x^*_{\mathbf{b}_2}(2)$	–	–	–	.06, .30	–
$x^*_{\mathbf{b}_2}(0), x^*_{\mathbf{b}_2}(2), A$	–	–	–	–	.09, .17

$$p_i(\varnothing) = \omega_i(0) \ \forall i, \tag{1}$$

constraints on the probabilities of non-empty sequences are:

$$p_i(q) = \sum_{a \ at \ h_q} p_i(q|a) \ \forall i, q \in Q_i, h_q \in I_q, \tag{2}$$

where I_q is the set of information sets reachable performing q, h_q is a information set belonging to I_q, a is an action available at information set h_q, and $q|a$ is the sequence obtained by adding action a to sequence q. Let consider $\mathbf{s}$ in Fig. 2, if $q = \langle x^*_{\mathbf{b}_1}(1) \rangle$, then the constraint (2) is $p_\mathbf{s}(q) = p_\mathbf{s}(\langle x^*_{\mathbf{b}_1}(1), A \rangle) + p_\mathbf{s}(\langle x^*_{\mathbf{b}_1}(1), x^*_{\mathbf{b}_1}(3) \rangle)$, because only one information set is reachable by performing q. The values of $\alpha(t)$ and $\beta(t)$ are easily computable on the basis of probability $p_i(q)$. More precisely, called q a $\mathbf{b}_w$'s sequence that ends at time point $t-1$ with $\iota(t) = \mathbf{b}$, we have $\alpha(t) = \frac{p_{\mathbf{b}_w}(q|x^*_{\mathbf{b}_s}(t))}{p_{\mathbf{b}_w}(q)}$. The values of $\beta(t)$ can be computed on the basis of $p_\mathbf{s}(q)$ in a similar way.

To solve the game we use the PNS algorithm [10] because it results very efficient: we can safely check a very small number of supports.

Theorem 42. *Excluded the degenerate case* $\omega_{\mathbf{b}_w}(0) = 1$, *agents' Nash equilibrium strategies on the equilibrium path in the reduced bargaining game are: if* $\iota(0) = \mathbf{b}$, *either* $\mathbf{b}_w$ *'s and* $\mathbf{s}$ *'s strategies are fully mixed or* $\mathbf{b}_w$ *makes offer*($x^*_{\mathbf{b}_s}(t)$) *with probability of 1 at* $t = 0$ *and* $\mathbf{s}$ *makes accept with probability of 1 at* $t = 1$; *if* $\iota(0) = \mathbf{s}$, *either* $\mathbf{s}$ *makes offer*($x^*_{\mathbf{b}_w}(0)$) *with probability of 1 at* $t = 0$ *and from* $t = 1$ *on* $\mathbf{b}_w$ *'s and* $\mathbf{s}$ *'s strategies are fully mixed or* $\mathbf{s}$ *makes offer*($x^*_{\mathbf{b}_s}(0)$) *with probability of 1 at* $t = 0$ *and* $\mathbf{b}_w$ *makes accept at* $t = 1$.

Proof. We show that on the equilibrium path $\mathbf{b}_w$ cannot make *accept* at time t with probability of 1 in all the decision nodes where multiple actions are available. Assume by contradiction that $\mathbf{b}_w$ makes it. Then, $\mathbf{s}$'s best response is to make *accept* at time $t + 1$ with probability of 1. However, if $\mathbf{s}$ makes such action at $t + 1$, $\mathbf{b}_w$'s best response is to make *offer*($x^*_{\mathbf{b}_s}(t)$) at time t and thus we have a contradiction. We show that on the equilibrium path $\mathbf{b}_w$ cannot make *offer*($x_{\mathbf{b}_s}(t)$) at time $t > 0$ with probability of 1 in all the decision nodes where multiple actions are available. Assume by contradiction that it happens. Then, $\mathbf{s}$'s best response is to make *accept* at time $t - 1$ with probability of 1. Therefore, time point t would never be reached on the equilibrium path and then we have a contradiction.

The same above reasoning can be applied to show that on the equilibrium path $\mathbf{s}$ cannot make with probability of 1 neither *accept* at time $t > 1$ nor *offer*($x_{\mathbf{b}_w}(t)$) at time $t > 0$. Thus, the unique possible agents' strategies on the equilibrium path are those reported in the theorem. If the fully mixed strategy is a Nash equilibrium, then it is by definition a sequential equilibrium. This is because every action is played with positive probability. If it is not an equilibrium, then necessarily the game concludes at $t = 1$.   □

The above theorem shows that for each bargaining problem we need to check only one joint support: if the fully mixed strategy is not an equilibrium, then on the equilibrium path the game concludes at $t = 1$. In this second case, to compute agents' equilibrium strategies off the equilibrium path it is sufficient to solve the reduced bargaining game from $t \geq 2$ with initial beliefs. The computational complexity of finding agents' equilibrium strategies on the equilibrium path is polynomial in $T_{\mathbf{b}_1}$, because the computational complexity of solving a linear feasibility problem is polynomial in the number of variables, this last number rises linearly in $T_{\mathbf{b}_1}$, and the number of joint supports to be checked is constant in the size of the game. Off the equilibrium path a number of joint supports that rises linearly in $T_{\mathbf{b}_1}$ must be checked, then the computational complexity is polynomial in $T_{\mathbf{b}_1}$. We use AMPL and CPLEX to solve the game. The computational times are negligible (< 1 s) even for large problems (up to $T_{\mathbf{b}_1} = 500$) with a 2.33 GHz 8 GB RAM UNIX computer. We report in Tab. 2 the values of $\alpha(t)$ and $\beta(t)$ for Example 31 with different values of initial beliefs.

Table 2. Values of $\alpha(t)$s and $\beta(t)$s. When $\omega_{\mathbf{b}_1}(0) = 0.1$ and $\omega_{\mathbf{b}_1}(0) = 0.7$ players always act in pure strategies; when $\omega_{\mathbf{b}_1}(0) = 0.8$ players randomize.

$\omega_{\mathbf{b}_1}(0)$	$\omega_{\mathbf{b}_2}(0)$	$\alpha(0)$	$\beta(1)$	$\alpha(2)$	$\beta(3)$
0.10	0.90	1.00	1.00	1.00	1.00
0.70	0.30	1.00	1.00	0.86	0.77
0.80	0.20	0.68	0.69	0.44	0.77

4.4   Extension to More Than Two Types

Here the idea is the same of the two–type solution. At first, we compute all the sequences of optimal offers $x^*_{\mathbf{b}_i}(t)$ in the complete–information games between $\mathbf{b}_i$ and $\mathbf{s}$. We rank the buyer's types from the strongest to the weakest according to $x^*_{\mathbf{b}_i}(0)$. At t each buyer's type $\mathbf{b}_i$ randomizes over all the offers $x^*_{\mathbf{b}_j}(t)$ such that $\mathbf{b}_j$ is not weaker than $\mathbf{b}_i$ and $\mathbf{b}_j$ is believed by $\mathbf{s}$ with positive probability. More precisely, we denote by $\alpha_{i,j}(t, \Theta_{\mathbf{b}}(t))$ the probability with which $\mathbf{b}_i$ makes offer $x^*_{\mathbf{b}_j}$ at time point t given that the buyer's types believed by $\mathbf{s}$ with strictly positive probability are those belonging to $\Theta_{\mathbf{b}}(t)$. Only the probabilities $\alpha_{i,j}(t, \Theta_{\mathbf{b}}(t))$ with $x^*_{\mathbf{b}_i}(t) > x^*_{\mathbf{b}_j}(t)$ and $\mathbf{b}_j \in \Theta_{\mathbf{b}}(t)$ can be non–null. The system of belief is such that, once offer $x^*_{\mathbf{b}_i}(t)$ is observed, all the types $\mathbf{b}_j$ with $x^*_{\mathbf{b}_j}(t) < x^*_{\mathbf{b}_i}(t)$ are removed from $\Theta_{\mathbf{b}}(t)$. Then, the number of possible $\Theta_{\mathbf{b}}(t)$ is linear in the size $\Theta_{\mathbf{b}}(0)$, e.g., if $\Theta_{\mathbf{b}}(0) = \{\mathbf{b}_1, \mathbf{b}_2, \mathbf{b}_3\}$, then the possible $\Theta_{\mathbf{b}}(t)$ are $\{\mathbf{b}_1, \mathbf{b}_2, \mathbf{b}_3\}$, $\{\mathbf{b}_2, \mathbf{b}_3\}$, and $\{\mathbf{b}_3\}$. Similarly, the seller's strategy can be represented by probabilities $\beta_j(t, \Theta_{\mathbf{b}}(t))$, i.e., the probability to accept $x^*_{\mathbf{b}_i}(t - 1)$/ offer $x^*_{\mathbf{b}_i}(t)$ at t when types $\Theta_{\mathbf{b}}(t)$ are believed with positive probabilities.

The construction of the game tree is accomplished according to the following rules: 1) no buyer's types makes offer strictly weaker than her optimal offer in the complete–information game; 2) at time $t > 0$, no agent (buyer and seller) makes offers strictly weaker (w.r.t. her utility function) than the one made by the opponent at the previous time point $t - 1$; 3) at time $t > 0$, no agent (buyer and seller) makes offers that, if accepted at $t + 1$, provide her the same utility she receives by accepting the offer made by the opponent at $t - 1$; 4) no buyer's type makes offers besides $\min\{T_{\mathbf{b}_i}, T_{\mathbf{s}}\}$ and the seller does not make offer besides $\min\{\max\{T_{\mathbf{b}_i}\}, T_{\mathbf{s}}\}$; 5) at time $t > 0$, an offer x_i is not made if the buyer's type $\mathbf{b}_i$ is out of the game (i.e., $t >= T_{\mathbf{b}_i}$ or type $\mathbf{b}_i$ has been excluded because the buyer has previously made an offer strictly weaker than the optimal complete–information offer of $\mathbf{b}_i$).

It can be easily observed that the size of the tree rises exponentially in the length of the deadlines. Differently from what we did for the two–type case, here do not use support–enumeration techniques, but we resort to linear–complementarity mathematical programming. This is because the number of supports rises as 4^n where n is the number of agents' actions, while the space of solutions over which linear complementarity works rises as 2.6^n.

We implemented an *ad hoc* version of the Lemke's algorithm with perturbation as described in [9] to compute a sequential equilibrium. The algorithm is based on pivoting (similarly to the simplex algorithm) where perturbation affects only the choice of the leaving variable. We coded the algorithm in C language by using integer pivoting and the same approach of the revised simplex (to save time during the update of the rows of the tableau). We executed our algorithm with a 2.33 GHz 8 GB RAM UNIX computer. We produced several bargaining instances characterized by the number of buyer's types (from 2 up to 6) and the deadline $T = \min\{\max\{T_{\mathbf{b}_i}\}, T_{\mathbf{s}}\}$ (from 6 up to 500). Tab. 3 reports the average computational times over 10 different bargaining instances; we denote by '–' the cases whose execution exceeds one hour.

Table 3. Computational times for solving a bargaining game with linear complementarity mathematical programming ($T = \min\{\max\{T_{\mathbf{b}_i}\}, T_{\mathbf{s}}\}$)

T	number of buyer's types				
	2	3	4	5	6
6	< 0.01 s	0.06 s	0.29 s	3.47 s	929.73 s
8	< 0.01 s	1.32 s	32.94 s	1890.96 s	–
10	< 0.01 s	15.16 s	2734.29 s	–	–
12	< 0.01 s	211.11 s	–	–	–
14	< 0.01 s	3146.20 s	–	–	–
50	0.22 s	–	–	–	–
100	1.55 s	–	–	–	–
500	175.90 s	–	–	–	–

As it can be observed, the computational times are exponential in the bargaining length and have the number of types as basis and only small settings can be solved by using linear–complementarity mathematical programming. Notice that the support–enumeration approach used for the two–types case is much faster than the linear–complementarity approach. This pushes for the development of algorithms for finding approximate solutions.

5   Conclusions and Future Works

The study of strategic bargaining with uncertainty is a challenging game theoretic problem. The literature provides several heuristics–based approaches generally applicable to any uncertain setting, while the optimal approaches work only with very narrow uncertainty settings. In particular, no algorithm works with uncertainty over multiple parameters. In this paper, we focused on one–sided uncertainty. Our main result is the reduction of the bargaining to a finite game. This allows one to resort to well known techniques to solve finite games. We proved that with two types the problem is polynomial (by using support–enumeration techniques), while with more types our algorithm requires exponential time. As a result, only small settings can be solved in exact way. Nevertheless, our reduction allows one to resort to techniques to find approximate equilibria.

In future works, on the one hand, we shall develop algorithms to find an ϵ–approximate equilibrium with a provable bound over ϵ and, on the other hand, we characterize solutions to produce insight over the structure of the problem and design more efficient exact algorithms.

References

1. Chatterjee, K., Samuelson, L.: Bargaining under two-sided incomplete information: The unrestricted offers case. Oper. Res. 36(4), 605–618 (1988)
2. Di Giunta, F., Gatti, N.: Bargaining over multiple issues in finite horizon alternating-offers protocol. Ann. Math. Artif. Intel. 47(3-4), 251–271 (2006)
3. Faratin, P., Sierra, C., Jennings, N.R.: Negotiation decision functions for autonomous agents. Robot. Auton. Syst. 24(3-4), 159–182 (1998)
4. Fatima, S.S., Wooldridge, M.J., Jennings, N.R.: On Efficient Procedures for Multi-issue Negotiation. In: Fasli, M., Shehory, O. (eds.) TADA/AMEC 2006. LNCS (LNAI), vol. 4452, pp. 31–45. Springer, Heidelberg (2007)
5. Gatti, N., Di Giunta, F., Marino, S.: Alternating-offers bargaining with one-sided uncertain deadlines: an efficient algorithm. Artif. Intell. 172(8-9), 1119–1157 (2008)
6. Gneezy, U., Haruvy, E., Roth, A.E.: Bargaining under a deadline: Evidence from the reverse ultimatum game. Game Econ. Behav. 45, 347–368 (2003)
7. Koller, D., Megiddo, N., von Stengel, B.: Efficient computation of equilibria for extensive two-person games. Game Econ. Behav. 14(2), 220–246 (1996)
8. Kreps, D.R., Wilson, R.: Sequential equilibria. Econometrica 50(4), 863–894 (1982)
9. Miltersen, P.B., Sorensen, T.B.: Computing sequential equilibria for two-player games. In: SODA, pp. 107–116 (2006)
10. Porter, R., Nudelman, E., Shoham, Y.: Simple search methods for finding a Nash equilibrium. In: AAAI, pp. 664–669 (2004)
11. Rubinstein, A.: Perfect equilibrium in a bargaining model. Econometrica 50(1), 97–109 (1982)
12. Rubinstein, A.: A bargaining model with incomplete information about time preferences. Econometrica 53(5), 1151–1172 (1985)
13. Rubinstein, A.: Choice of conjectures in a bargaining game with incomplete information. In: Roth, A.E. (ed.) Game-Theoretic Models of Bargaining, pp. 99–114. Cambridge University Press, Cambridge (1985)
14. Sandholm, T.: Agents in electronic commerce: Component technologies for automated negotiation and coalition formation. Auton. Agent Multi-AG 3(1), 73–96 (2000)

An Adaptive Proportional Value-per-Click Agent for Bidding in Ad Auctions

Kyriakos C. Chatzidimitriou[1,2], Lampros C. Stavrogiannis[3],
Andreas L. Symeonidis[1,2], and Pericles A. Mitkas[1,2]

[1] Department of Electrical and Computer Engineering,
Aristotle University of Thessaloniki, Greece
[2] Informatics and Telematics Institute,
Centre for Research and Technology Hellas, Greece
[3] School of Electronics and Computer Science
University of Southampton, UK
mertacor@olympus.ee.auth.gr

Abstract. Sponsored search auctions constitutes the most important source of revenue for search engine companies, offering new opportunities for advertisers. The Trading Agent Competition (TAC) Ad Auctions tournament is one of the first attempts to study the competition among advertisers for their placement in sponsored positions along with organic search engine results. In this paper, we describe agent Mertacor, a simulation-based game theoretic agent coupled with on-line learning techniques to optimize its behavior that successfully competed in the 2010 tournament. In addition, we evaluate different facets of our agent to draw conclusions about certain aspects of its strategy.

Keywords: sponsored search, advertisement auction, trading agent, game theory, machine learning.

1 Introduction

The advent of the Internet has radically altered current business landscape. One of its prominent applications is on-line advertising in search engine results, known as sponsored search, where paid advertisements are shown along with regular results (called impressions). Sponsored search is the highest source of revenue for on-line advertisement, yielding a profit of approximately $10.67 billions for 2009 only in the U.S. [1].

In the sponsored search setting, whenever a user enters a query in the search engine (publisher), an auction is run among interested advertisers, who must select the amount of their bids, as well as the advertisements that they deem to be more relevant to the user. There is a number of positions (slots) for placement, but higher slots are more desirable, given that they generally yield higher levels of Click-Through-Rate (CTR). This field started in 1998 by GoTo.com, where slots were allocated via a Generalized First Price (GFP) auction, but received its current form in 2002, when GFP was replaced by the well known Generalized Second Price (GSP) auction [2]. According to this auction, bids are sorted by bid (that is usually multiplied by an advertiser-specific quality factor), and the winner of a slot pays the minimum bid needed to get this position, which is slightly

E. David et al. (Eds.): AMEC/TADA 2011, LNBIP 119, pp. 15–27, 2013.

higher than the next bidder's offer and independent of her bid. What makes this type of auctions different is the fact that payment is made on a per click (cost-per-click or CPC) rather than a per impression (cost-per-mille or CPM) basis.

Against this background, we present the strategy of agent *Mertacor*, our entrant that participated in the TAC Ad Auctions 2010 competition [3] and was placed 3rd in the finals. At a high level, Mertacor's strategy can be decomposed into two parts: (a) estimating the Value-per-Click (VPC) for each query and (b) choosing a proportion of VPC for bidding in each auction based on the state of the game (the adaptive proportional part). The approach is similar to the QuakTAC agent [4], which participated in the 2009 competition, with two extensions: (a) a k-nearest-neighbors algorithm to help in the estimation of VPC and (b) an associative to the state of the game, n-armed bandit formulation of the problem of selecting the proportion of VPC to bid.

The remainder of this paper is organized as follows: Section 2 provides a brief description of the game. Section 3 presents strategies of agents participated in the previous competition. Section 4 builds the background upon which our agent was based and gives a detailed description of the extension points. A discussion of the conducted experiments is given in Section 5. Finally, Section 6 concludes the paper and provides our future research directions.

2   The TAC Ad Auctions Game

Sponsored search auctions are open, highly complex mechanisms, that are non-dominant-strategy-solvable, hence bidding strategies are a topic of active research. To investigate their behavior, a realistic agent-based simulator seems essential [5]. The Ad Auctions (AA) platform in the international Trading Agent Competition (TAC) is such a system. The TAC AA game specifications are defined in detail in [3]. To familiarize the reader with the game, we will provide some basic information about the entities involved and the interactions between them.

In TAC AA tournament, there are three main types of entities: the `publisher`, a population of 90000 `users`, and eight `advertiser` entrants represented by autonomous software agents. The advertisers compete against each other for advertisement (ad) placement, across search pages. Each one of the search pages contains search engine results for one of the queries of 16 different keyword sets. In order to promote their products, the agents participate in ad auctions by submitting a bid and an ad to the publisher for the query (set of keywords) they are interested in. Ads are ranked on each search page, based on a generalized method that interpolates between rank-by-bid and rank-by-revenue schemes. Each day, users, according to their preferences and state, remain idle, search, click on ads and make purchases (conversions) from the advertisers' websites. The products being traded are combinations of three brands and three types of components from the domain of home entertainment. The small number of products enables competing teams to focus only on a small set of predefined keywords, abstracting away from the problems of keyword selection. The three manufacturers (namely, Lioneer, PG and Flat) and the three types of devices (TV, Audio and DVD) constitute a total of nine products. The simulation runs over 60 virtual days, with each day lasting 10 seconds. A schematic of the interactions between game entities is found in Figure 1.

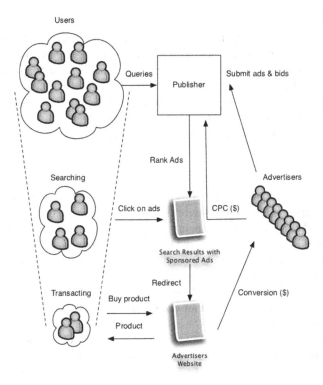

Fig. 1. The entities participating in a TAC AA game along with their actions. The majority of the users submit queries, fewer click on ads and an even smaller percentage makes transactions.

2.1 Advertisers

Each advertiser is a retailer of home entertainment products and can supply the user with any of the nine products available. Upon initialization of each simulation, advertisers are given a component and a manufacturer specialty, yielding an increase in conversion rates for the former and an increase in profit per unit sold for the later. Additionally, entrants are assigned a weekly maximum stock capacity $C^{cap} \in \{C^{LOW}, C^{MED}, C^{HIGH}\}$, so conversions above this threshold are less likely to happen during this week (5 working days). During its daily cycle of activities the advertiser agent on day d has to:

- Send the bids for ad placement per query for day $d + 1$.
- Select an ad for ad placement per query for day $d + 1$. The ad can be either generic (i.e. referring to a general electronics shop) or targeted (i.e. stating a specific manufacturer-component combination). A targeted ad that is a match to the user preferences increases the probability of clicking that ad.
- Set spending limits for each query and across all queries for day $d + 1$.
- Receive reports about the market and its campaign for day $d - 1$.

2.2   Publishers

As mentioned above, the publisher runs a GSP auction to determine the rank of bids and determine the payment per click. The ad placement algorithm takes into account predefined reserve scores. There is one reserve score, below which, an ad will not be posted, and one above which, an ad will be promoted. If the spending limit set by an agent is passed, the rankings are recalculated. The auction implemented is a GSP, where the ranking takes into account the quality of the advertisements, weighted by a squashing parameter that is disclosed to the entrants at the beginning of the game.

2.3   Users

Each user has a unique product preference and can be in different states representing his or her searching and buying behavior (i.e. non-searching, informational searching, shopping, with distinct levels of shopping focus, and transacted). The product preference distribution is even for all products. Users submit three kinds of queries, defined by their focus level for a total of 16 queries. There is one (1) $F0$ query, where no manufacturer or component preference is revealed, six (6) $F1$ queries, where only the manufacturer or the product type is included in the query and nine (9) $F2$ queries, where the full product definition (manufacturer and type) is exposed. Users' daily state transition is modeled as a Markov chain. Non-searching and transacted agents do not submit queries. Informational agents submit one of the three queries by selecting any one of the them uniformly and focused users submit a query depending on their focus level. While both information seeking and focused users could click on an ad, only focused users make purchases and go to the transacted state. Users click on the advertisements based on an extended version of the cascade model [6]. After clicking on an ad, whether a conversion will be made or not depends on user's state, advertisers' specialty and remaining distribution capacity.

3   Related Work

Given that the tournament started in 2009, relevant published work on TAC AA is limited. The majority of strategies is focused on two target metrics, namely the *Return on Investment* (ROI), i.e. the ratio of profit to cost, and the *Value per Click* (VPC), i.e. the expected profit from a conversion given a click, and combined with multiple choice knapsack (MCKP) models to deal with the distribution constraint effect.

TacTex [7], the winner of the previous competitions, implements a two-stage strategy of estimation and optimization. The former incorporates self and opponent related predictions of desired variables as well as user state estimation. More specifically, this agent tries to extract the range of impressions, ranking and amount of bids, as well as the type of ads shown. Then, it estimates the proportion of users in each state and utilizes this information to predict the most profitable number of conversions per query type. The optimization takes into consideration the distribution constraint effect, hence both short-term and long-term optimizers are incorporated in the strategy. Finally, there is an estimator for the unknown game parameters, i.e. continuation probability and quality factor.

Another competitor for 2009, *Schlemazl*, employs rule-based as well as dynamic programming techniques. According to the latter, the bidding process is modeled as a penalized MCKP, where the value of each query is the profit made and the weight is the number of sales [8]. For the rule-based method, the agent's strategy targets for the same ROI in all queries. A similar principle is implemented in *EPFLAgent 2010* [9], targeting for the same profit per conversion over all queries, and distributes the number of sales uniformly on the five most recent days. If the number of sales exceeds this threshold, the bid for the most profitable keyword is increased, otherwise the bid on the least profitable keyword is decreased.

Tau [10] follows a reinforcement learning (soft greedy) approach, based on regret minimization, where the agent selects a value from a distribution on the space of bids, so that the regret, which is the difference between actual profit and maximum profit, is minimized. On the other hand, *DNAgent* [11] follows an evolutionary computation technique, by creating a population of agents (referred as finite state machines) that are genetically evolved until the fittest is determined. Each agent can be in seven different states, based on its previous position, which is combined with the matching of the advertisement to the user to determine bid adjustments for the next day.

Finally, *AstonTAC* [12] and *QuakTAC* [4] follow VPC-based strategies. The former estimates the market VPC, which is the VPC minus relevant cost, and then bids a proportion of this value based on the critical capacity (i.e. capacity beyond which the expected cost is higher than the corresponding revenue) and the estimated quality factor for the advertiser. Priority is also given to the most profitable queries. On the other hand, QuakTAC follows a simulation based Bayes-Nash equilibrium estimation technique to find the optimum percentage of the VPC to bid. One important advantage of the VPC strategy is that it does not require any opponent modeling techniques, which in turn, demand historical information about opponents' bidding behavior, difficult to obtain in reality.

4 Agent Mertacor

4.1 Background

The baseline strategy of agent Mertacor is a modified version of the aforementioned QuakTAC strategy for the 2009 tournament [4]. This is one of the few reported strategies in TAC that employs simulation based game theoretic analysis and was proven quite successful in that tournament, as QuakTAC was placed 4th in the finals. It is a sound, elegant and yet simple strategy. For the bidding part, Vorobeychik considers a simple strategy space, with bids that are linear to the valuation of the player. For the AA scenario, this valuation is the advertiser's VPC, v, and the agent bids a proportion (shading), α, of this value. For each query q, the bid for day $d + 1$ would be:

$$bid_{d+1}^q = \alpha \cdot v_{d+1}^q \tag{1}$$

Given that GSP auctions are not incentive compatible [13], we expect that $\alpha < 1$. An estimation of the VPC for a keyword can be expressed as the product of the probability of converting after a click on the ad and the expected revenue from such a conversion. So for each query q, the agent's estimated VPC value can be calculated as:

$$\widehat{v}^q = \widehat{Pr}^q\{conversion|click\} \cdot E[revenue^q|conversion] \qquad (2)$$

The expected revenue for a query q given a conversion, ($E[revenue^q|conversion]$), solely depends on the advertiser's Manufacturer Specialty (MS) and can be calculated with no additional information for the three possible cases as follows:

$$\begin{cases} (USP \cdot (3 + MSB))/3 & \text{MS not defined in } q \\ USP \cdot (1 + MSB) & \text{MS matched in } q \\ USP & \text{MS not matched in } q \end{cases} \qquad (3)$$

where USP is the unit sales profit ($10 in TAC 2010) and MSB the manufacturer specialty bonus (0.4 in TAC 2010).

However, for calculating the probability of conversion, we need two additional estimations, the proportion of focused users and past and future conversions that have an impact on the conversion probability due to the distribution constraint effect:

$$\widehat{Pr}^q_{d+1}\{conversion|click\} = focused\widehat{Percentage}^q \cdot$$
$$Pr^q\{conversion|focused\}(\hat{I}_{d+1}) \qquad (4)$$

To calculate a value for the $focused\widehat{Percentage}^q$ estimate, we used the following procedure. If we fix advertisers' policies, then the proportion of focused users is equal to the ratio of the clicks that result in conversions divided by their individual probability of conversion (incorporating the distribution constraint effect). The user population model in TAC AA is a Markov chain and, despite the incorporation of the burst transitions, it will typically converge to a stationary distribution. Hence, instead of using a more sophisticated and accurate particle filter, we have used Monte Carlo simulations, running 100 games with symmetric, fixed strategy profiles, making sure that their bids are always higher than those requested by reserve scores, and have then recorded the mean values for our desired ratios (every day results for individual queries are aggregated for each focus level). Historical proportions are kept in log files and are updated incrementally. In our experiments, we have used last day's probability of conversion as a close estimate of the requested value for the denominator.

Our first differentiation compared to the original strategy lies in the estimation of the conversion probability, $Pr^q\{conversion|focused\}(\hat{I}_{d+1})$, which is a function of the distribution constraint effect, I_d. As Jordan has noticed in his thesis [14], the distribution constraint effect, I_d, is the second most influential factor in an advertiser's performance after the manufacturer specialty in terms of the coefficient of determination values. This effect radically affects the probability of purchase. Based on the specifications of the game for the calculation of the distribution constraint effect for day $d + 1$, we need, but don't have the conversions, c, of day d and $d + 1$:

$$I_{d+1} = g(c_{d-3} + c_{d-2} + c_{d-1} + \hat{c}_d + \hat{c}_{d+1} - C^{cap}) \qquad (5)$$

where g is a function defined in the specification that gives the value of I_d.

Given that an entrant must calculate a bid with a 2-day lag in available information, QuakTAC estimates tomorrow's I_{d+1} value using a two-step bootstrapping technique. More specifically, it estimates conversions on day d as the product of current game's historical click-through rate, recorded historical impressions and (optimistically) estimated conversion probability. Then it uses this information to estimate day's $d + 1$ conversion rate and corresponding conversions and uses an averaged value for the I_{d+1}.

Having implemented that strategy, we realized that it performs poorly on the 2010 server specifications. It seems that it underestimates the VPC, systematically bidding much lower than what is allowed by the publisher's reserve scores. It is important to note that these scores for 2010 are much higher than 2009. Jordan describes the effect of the reserve score on publisher's revenue as well as players' equilibrium showing that AstonTAC and Schlemazl perform much better than TacTex for these higher reserve scores. To rectify this shortcoming, we have implemented a simpler but more reasonable expectation: we aggregate last three days' conversions and set $\frac{1}{4}$ of this value as our number of conversions for day d as well as day $d + 1$. This is slightly lower than their corresponding mean value so as to intentionally be more conservative. However, when our capacity is C^{LOW}, we have used instead the mean value, which was experimentally shown to yield better results in this case.

Finally, we had to select the percentage of our VPC to bid. Following the methodology of Vorobeychik, we restrict our interest in simple symmetric equilibria and discrete values ranging from 0 to 1 with a step of 0.1. This means that all but one advertisers follow the same strategy ($bid = \alpha v$) and a single player bids another α_{single} percentage, which varies among games. The values for α_{single} are determined via an iterative best response method, where we start from a truthful homogeneous strategy profile ($\alpha = 1$, $\alpha_{single} = 1$). This is a reasonable value to start, as GSP is considered a generalization of the Vickrey auction. Then we find the best α_{single} deviation from this profile and use this last value as the new homogeneous profile. This process is repeated until self-response is a Bayes-Nash equilibrium. We have validated the speed of this method, being able to get the best value of $\alpha_{single} = 0.3$ in three iterations (1, 0.4 and 0.3). The alpha value of 0.3 and the new method for calculating I_d are the differentiation we made to the agent playing in the qualifications round of TAC AA 2010 and further defined as *Mertacor-Quals*.

Ad Selection Strategy. It is also important to describe our ad selection strategy. This task is straightforward for $F0$ (no keywords) and $F2$ (containing both brand and product keywords) type queries. For the first case, there is a $\frac{1}{9}$ probability of matching a user's preference, so a generic ad seems most appropriate. On the other hand, users reveal truthfully their preferences, hence a targeted $F2$ ad will always match them. For the $F1$ keywords (containing either brand or product keywords), we have also used a targeted advertisement, where our agent's respective specialty is shown when the manufacturer or the component are not disclosed, hoping that our increased profit or conversion probability benefits will outweigh our higher probabilities of mismatch. This strategy also proved to be effective in the original QuakTAC agent [4].

4.2 Extensions

For the final rounds, we tried to improve our agent in the two critical calculations of: a) estimating the distribution constraint effect and b) finding an appropriate α value by adapting it on-line according to the current market conditions.

In the first case, we used the k-Nearest-Neighbors (k-NN) algorithm to estimate the capacity to be committed for the current day c_d and then using that estimate to further predict the capacity to be purchased on day c_{d+1}. We chose $k = 5$ and stored 5-day tuples for the last 10 games (600 samples). We adopted this kind of modeling because the agent executes a clear 5-day cycle in its bidding and conversion behavior. This behavior is derived from the strategy of the agent since when having enough remaining capacity, it will produce high bids due to high VPC values and get ranked in the first positions. That way it will receive many clicks and a high volume of conversions will take place. This behavior will continue for one more day, until the agent's store is depleted. Then the bids will be low and the agent will maintain a no conversions status for three days.

In order to choose the proportion of the VPC to bid in a real antagonistic environment, we have formulated the problem of choosing α into an associative n-armed bandit problem [15]. Under this formulation, we switched bidding from $b(v) = \alpha \cdot v$ to $b(\alpha, v) = \alpha \cdot v$.

Based on the experience gained from the TAC Supply Chain Management domain, we tried to maintain a low dimensionality in the state and action spaces for sampling efficiency. We chose VPC and query types as a state variables. The choice of VPC was made because its calculation incorporates many parameters that characterize the state of the agent and the market such as: specialties, distribution capacity constraint, and proportion of focused users. The query type was added as state variable in order to provide additional information about the current state from another dimension. VPC was quantized over 11 states, 10 for VPC values between \$0 and \$10 and 1 for VPC values above \$10. The 16 query types were mapped into 8 states as presented in Table 1. There were 6 discrete actions picking values of α between equal spaced points from 0.275 to 0.325 inclusive. So a total of 528 Q(s,a) values need to be stored and updated. For exploration purposes ϵ-greedy policy was used with $\epsilon = 0.1$. The goal is to learn a policy for selecting one of the 6 actions that would maximize the daily profit given the state of the game. Updates to Q values were made using the learning rule:

$$Q(s, a)_{k+1} = Q(s, a)_k + 0.1 \cdot (r_k - Q(s, a)_k) \tag{6}$$

Reward is the daily profit calculate as the revenue minus the cost for the corresponding state and action.

$$r = revenue - CPC \cdot \#clicks \tag{7}$$

On day d we receive the report for day $d - 1$ from which we can calculate the reward for day $d - 1$. That reward concerns the bids made on day $d - 2$ for day $d - 1$.

5   Analysis

To validate the effectiveness of this iterative best response technique, after the tournament we have also repeated the experiments for all possible combinations of homogeneous and single α values and have plotted the best α_{single} as a function of the

Table 1. Mapping query types to states. One state for the $F0$ query, 3 states for $F1$ queries and 4 states for $F2$ queries

Query Type	State ID
F0	1
F1 with no matching specialty	2
F1 with matching manufacturer specialty	3
F1 with matching component specialty	4
F2 with no matching specialty	5
F2 with matching manufacturer specialty	6
F2 with matching component specialty	7
F2 with all matching specialties	8

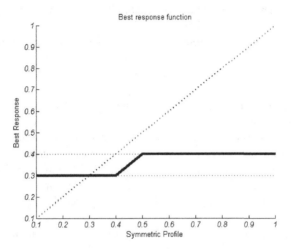

Fig. 2. Best response function

symmetric opponent profile. Each experiment was repeated 5 times for a total of 500 log files. Results are given in Figure 2. As can be seen, there are only two close values for $\alpha_{single}(0.3, 0.4)$, although 0.3 is best response for more reasonable strategies ($\alpha < 0.5$). Hence, this technique yields robust results in only 3% of total required time for extensive experiments. Moreover, we should note that the values of 0.1 and 0.2 used by QuakTAC last year are not profitable at all in this year's platform due to the aforementioned reserve score effect.

The final version of agent Mertacor got the third place in the TAC AA 2010 competition. The standings are shown in Table 2.

To evaluate the effectiveness of the agent and the extensions incorporated, two tournaments were conducted. Four versions of agent Mertacor were constructed. *Mertacor-Quals* is the agent that participated in the qualifications of the 2010 tournament. *Mertacor-kNN* has only the k-NN capability, while it continues to bid with

Table 2. TAC AA 2010 tournament results

Position	Agent	Average Score ($)
1	TacTex	58 130
2	Schlemazl	52 868
3	**Mertacor**	52 383
4	MetroClick	52 210
5	Nanda_AA	48 084
6	crocodileagent	47 779
7	tau	44 419
8	McCon	43 415

$\alpha = 0.3$. *Mertacor-RL* has the ability to adapt α, but is not equipped with k-NN. Last but not least, *Mertacor-Finals* combines all the modifications and extensions described in this paper and is the agent participated in the 2010 finals. In the first tournament, two agents from each one of the four versions of the agent competed, having all the same storage capacity equal to C^{MED}. In the second tournament the storage capacities were selected in competition terms (2 agents with C^{LOW}, 4 with C^{MED} and 2 with C^{HIGH}).

Results in Table 3 indicate that the extension added to the Mertacor-Finals version of the agent is giving the agent a small boost. Both versions were able to get the first two positions in this tournament. Even though the differences are not large enough and not statistical significant under paired t-testing, in tightly played competitions they could make the difference over ranking positions, like in 2010. Moreover, we believe that by optimizing these techniques, now implemented rather crudely, more profit is possible. It is also evident that including both extensions has more benefits than anyone of them alone.

When dealing with different capacities between games, the domain becomes more challenging, especially for on-line learning methods. In Table 4, one can find the results of the second tournament. Again the differences are not large enough, but there are small deviations between versions. The k-NN version is able to estimate better the capacity

Table 3. Average scores over 88 games of different versions of agent Mertacor with equal distribution capacity constraint $C = C^{MED}$

Agent	Mean Score	Aggregate Score
Mertacor-Quals-1	$53 330	$53 036
Mertacor-Quals-2	$52 742	
Mertacor-kNN-1	$53 575	$53 151
Mertacor-kNN-2	$52 727	
Mertacor-RL-1	$53 006	$52 959
Mertacor-RL-2	$52 912	
Mertacor-Finals-1	**$53 819**	**$53 806**
Mertacor-Finals-2	$53 793	

to be used by the agent and this benefits the final scoring of the agent In Figure 3, one can obverse the quality of the k-NN predictions. It is possible that by optimizing this algorithm, extremely accurate results could be possible. As general comment, all versions of the agent, in both tournaments, were able to maintain their bank accounts to the level agent Mertacor scored in the finals. This is evidence of a robust strategy against both similar and different opponents.

Table 4. Average scores over 88 games of different versions of agent Mertacor in competition mode with respect to distribution capacity constraints

Agent	Mean Score	Aggregate Score
Mertacor-Quals-1	$53 679	$53 289
Mertacor-Quals-2	$52 900	
Mertacor-kNN-1	**$54 632**	**$53 998**
Mertacor-kNN-2	$53 365	
Mertacor-RL-1	$52 712	$53 271
Mertacor-RL-2	$53 831	
Mertacor-Finals-1	$53 615	$53 334
Mertacor-Finals-2	$53 054	

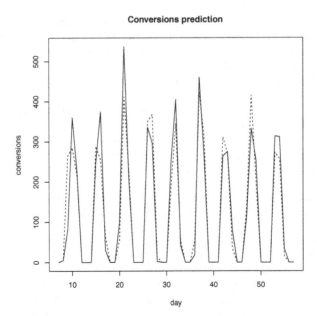

Fig. 3. k-NN enabled predictions of conversions for the future day (dashed line). The solid line indicates the actual conversions made.

6   Conclusions and Future Work

In this report we have described our agent, *Mertacor*, for the TAC AA 2010 tournament. We have seen how empirical game theory can provide robust and effective results in a restricted real-world setting, when operationalized appropriately using simple abstractions. We were also able to discuss about the importance of the distribution constraint effect and the reserve score in our results, which significantly influenced our agent's performance before and during the tournament. Last but not least, we have elaborated on two extensions, k-nearest neighbors and reinforcement learning that differentiate our agent from related work and provide added value to the agent with respect to making better predictions and adapting to the environment and the competition.

As future work, we would first need to use a more accurate user state predictor, such as the one implemented by TacTex. Moreover, we would like to extend our strategy to quadratic functions of the VPC, to incorporate the decrease in α for smaller corresponding valuations [16], as was also implemented in QuakTAC during the finals of 2009. Other non-linear function approximators could also be tested, under off-line parameter learning schemes for boosting time to converge to an optimal policy. Finally, it would be desirable to identify key parameters that influence more or less the optimal bidding percentage.

References

1. PwC: IAB U.S. Internet Advertising Revenue Report for 2009 (April 2010)
2. Jansen, B.J., Mullen, T.: Sponsored search: an overview of the concept, history, and technology. International Journal of Electronic Business 6(2), 114–131 (2008)
3. Jordan, P.R., Cassell, B., Callender, L.F., Kaul, A., Wellman, M.P.: The ad auctions game for the 2010 trading agent competition. Technical report, University of Michigan, Ann Arbor, MI 48109-2121 USA (2010)
4. Vorobeychik, Y.: A Game Theoretic Bidding Agent for the Ad Auction Game. In: Third International Conference on Agents and Artificial Intelligence, ICAART 2011 (January 2011)
5. Feldman, J., Muthukrishnan, S.: Algorithmic methods for sponsored search advertising. In: Liu, Z., Xia, C.H. (eds.) Performance Modeling and Engineering (2008)
6. Das, A., Goitis, I., Karlin, A.R., Mathieu, C.: On the effects of competing advertisements in keyword auctions. Working Paper (2008)
7. Pardoe, D., Chakraborty, D., Stone, P.: TacTex09: A champion bidding agent for ad auctions. In: Proceedings of the 9th International Conference on Autonomous Agents and Multiagent Systems (AAMAS 2010) (May 2010)
8. Berg, J., Greenwald, A., Naroditskiy, V., Sodomka, E.: A knapsack-based approach to bidding in ad auctions. In: Proceeding of the 2010 Conference on ECAI 2010: 19th European Conference on Artificial Intelligence, pp. 1013–1014. IOS Press, Amsterdam (2010)
9. Cigler, L., Mirza, E.: EPFLAgent: A Bidding Strategy for TAC/AA. Presentation in Workshop on Trading Agent Design and Analysis (TADA), ACM EC 2010 (July 2010)
10. Mansour, Y., Schain, M.: TAU Agent. Presentation in Workshop on Trading Agent Design and Analysis (TADA), ACM EC 2010 (July 2010)
11. Munsey, M., Veilleux, J., Bikkani, S., Teredesai, A., De Cock, M.: Born to trade: A genetically evolved keyword bidder for sponsored search. In: 2010 IEEE Congress on Evolutionary Computation (CEC), pp. 1–8 (2010)

12. Chang, M., He, M., Luo, X.: Designing a successful adaptive agent for tac ad auction. In: Proceeding of the 2010 Conference on ECAI 2010: 19th European Conference on Artificial Intelligence, pp. 587–592. IOS Press, Amsterdam (2010)
13. Lahaie, S.: An analysis of alternative slot auction designs for sponsored search. In: EC 2006: Proceedings of the 7th ACM Conference on Electronic Commerce, pp. 218–227. ACM, New York (2006)
14. Jordan, P.R.: Practical Strategic Reasoning with Applications in Market Games. PhD thesis, University of Michigan, Ann Arbor, MI (2010)
15. Sutton, R.S., Barto, A.G.: Reinforcement Learning: An Introduction. MIT Press, Cambridge (1998)
16. Vorobeychik, Y.: Simulation-based game theoretic analysis of keyword auctions with low-dimensional bidding strategies. In: Twenty-Fifth Conference on Uncertainty in Articial Intelligence (2009)

Improving Prediction in TAC SCM by Integrating Multivariate and Temporal Aspects via PLS Regression

William Groves and Maria Gini

University of Minnesota
Department of Computer Science and Engineering
Minneapolis, MN 55455 USA
{groves,gini}@cs.umn.edu

Abstract. We address the construction of a prediction model from data available in a complex environment. We first present a data extraction method that is able to leverage information contained in the movements of all variables in recent observations. This improved data extraction is then used with a common multivariate regression technique: Partial Least Squares (PLS) regression. We experimentally validate this combined data extraction and modeling with data from a competitive multi-agent supply chain setting, the Trading Agent Competition for Supply Chain Management (TAC SCM). Our method achieves competitive (and often superior) performance compared to the state-of-the-art domain-specific prediction techniques used in the 2008 Prediction Challenge competition.

Keywords: prediction, price modeling, feature selection, regression, machine learning.

1 Introduction

The basic purpose of prediction in decision making scenarios is to provide information about the future that is relevant to decisions that must be made now. In a supply chain scenario, prediction is generally concerned with providing information about future costs, prices, and demand so that decisions can be made today that maximize utility. Other aspects such as limited information, informational delays, changing conditions, and observation noise can add complexity to the environment and make prediction more difficult. The Trading Agent Competition for Supply Chain Management (TAC SCM) is a market simulation game that possesses all these challenges.

TAC SCM is a complex, heterogeneous-agent supply chain game that is designed to simulate an oligopoly market of competing computer manufacturing agents who must autonomously purchase component parts, manufacture computers, and sell the finished computers to end customers over a simulated product lifetime of a year. Each run of the simulation, which takes approximately one hour in real-time, is unique because the market's behavior will vary both due to changes in the underlying market conditions (available component supply and customer demand), and due to changes in the behavior of individual agents. This competition, which has been held annually since 2003, has attracted many participants from around the world [1].

E. David et al. (Eds.): AMEC/TADA 2011, LNBIP 119, pp. 28–43, 2013.

For the purposes of this paper, we are primarily concerned with the price prediction aspects of the competition. A subcompetition called the "Prediction Challenge" was initiated in 2007 to isolate this aspect of the simulation for study [2]. This subcompetition facilitated direct comparisons of prediction performance on four prediction types: (1) current product prices, (2) future product prices, (3) current component prices, and (4) future component prices. "Current" refers to predictions about prices revealed to an agent on the next day; "future" refers to predictions about prices revealed to an agent an additional 20 days in the future from the current day. For each prediction class, we show how to generate an optimal feature set and the prediction results of PLS regression using these features.

The challenge of predicting in this environment is that many variables have relationships to other variables that are not easily quantified. Economic theory suggests that there is a direct relationship between the cost of parts and the cost of finished goods, but, in a situation where parts are shared across many products, the relationships are dynamic. Instead of modeling these relationships individually, we use partial least squares (PLS) regression, which is able to implicitly determine correlations between input variables based on historical data. To effectively model these relationships, a corpus of historical data is required to calibrate the model. The observations used to construct the training set features should be representative of the range of values the model will need to predict over. In a multi-agent setting, this means that the training data should be generated by a similar set of opponents as when predictions are to be made.

We make two novel contributions: (1) we include time-delayed observations as additional elements in the feature vector, in addition to the most recent observed value of each variable, and (2) we segment the features hierarchically into classes, based on their relationship to the variable of interest. Searching for the optimal combination of time-delayed features is done by varying independently for each class the depth of lagged data to be included in the feature vector. This makes the computation tractable and efficient. Despite the fact our method uses very little domain-knowledge, we achieved competitive (and often superior) performance compared to the domain-specific prediction techniques in the 2008 Prediction Challenge.

The paper is structured as follows: in the next section, we present related work relevant to PLS regression and previous prediction approaches used in TAC SCM. In Section 3, our data extraction and prediction methodology is outlined including how the feature vector is augmented to include data from past observations. Our prediction results are presented and compared with the state-of-the-art methods in Section 5. Section 6 concludes with a discussion of future work.

2   Background and Related Work

The majority of prediction models can be classified as one of two types: on-line (only information from a short window of recent observations is used) and off-line (significant volumes of historical data are used to calibrate the model). While on-line methods can be more robust to changes in the environment and can provide good performance in a dynamic environment, often better performance can be achieved by incorporating training on historical data. For these reasons, typically on-line models are tried first, and off-line models are used as higher performance becomes necessary.

The TAC SCM competition as well as other autonomous agent competitions require agents to do significant forecasting to achieve consistent, strong performance.

TAC SCM: Current and Future Product Prices. In TAC SCM component prices are the prices agents must pay when buying component parts. Product prices are the prices agents must be concerned with when selling their finished goods to end customers. There is a mismatch between the phases of buying components and selling products which is due to the fact that the lowest component costs are generally seen for orders for components with a long lead time (up to 220 days), which are far beyond the maximum lead time of the customer requests for finished computers (up to 12 days).

The prediction methods employed by top performers in the TAC SCM competition involve a combination of offline training on historical data for computation of latent (or not always visible) information. Overall, an agent has significant tactical reasons to estimate next day prices due to the need to assign a specific bid price for each customer request the agent wants to bid for.

The TacTex agent makes next day product price predictions using a particle filter to compute the lowest price offered by any agent in response to each request [3].

The Deep Maize agent uses a k-nearest neighbor technique over a large set of historical data. The feature vector, over which similarity is computed, includes current day estimates of supplier capacity (which features prominently in the pricing equation), today's observed customer demand, and recently observed computer prices [4]. This method explicitly limits the contribution of individual games by using only the most similar observation from each game in the data set.

The CMieux agent (an agent not participating in the prediction challenge) uses a decision tree variant called a distribution tree that tracks several distinct distributions of prices and chooses the most relevant normal distribution to use based on publicly known attributes of the price to estimate [5].

The MinneTAC agent (also not in the prediction challenge) uses a double exponential smoothing time series over the recently observed high and low price for each product type to estimate next day product prices [6]. A classification-based approach used in [7] involves clustering observed market behaviors into economic regimes to build both current and future product price distribution models.

For 20 day ahead sales price predictions ("future product"), most agents report to use methods similar to their next day approaches.

The TacTex agent uses the result of its next day particle filter and augments this value by computing an adjustment for 20 day ahead predictions using an additive regression model. The additive regression model estimates the difference between the next day price and the 20 day ahead price and is derived from a set of 31 visible features (16 product prices, 3 demand signals, storage cost, interest rate, and 10 unique component prices) from the current day's observations. This technique is similar to the PLS regression method discussed in Section 3 but differs by not using information observed prior to the current day.

Deep Maize estimates future product prices using the same k-nearest neighbor used in next day predictions but instead trained on 20 day ahead observations.

Some agents do not estimate 20 day ahead product prices at all because this prediction is not required when operating in TAC SCM. However, some agents use some form of long-term product price prediction to plan their long lead-time procurement.

TAC SCM: Current and Future Component Prices. A component request is priced depending on the amount of uncommitted factory capacity on the supply line between the current day and the delivery date. Prices are sensitive to the actions of the competing agents, since requests from other agents reduce the available capacity of the suppliers.

Component pricing is significantly more complex due to the need to consider lead time. When an agent makes a request for component parts it must also specify a delivery lead-time. This is critical because the prices quoted vary significantly over the range of possible lead times. Generally, the longest lead-time requests are the cheapest, but this is not always true. Interestingly, the lead-time aspect of product prices is not explicitly considered by many TAC SCM agents.

TacTex predicts next day component prices with a domain-specific approach by estimating the available production capacity of each supplier. This is done using knowledge of how component prices are calculated. The fraction of unallocated supplier capacity between the request date and the delivery date is directly proportional to the quoted per unit cost for each request. This value can be estimated by observing differences in the recent quoted prices. Note, however, that this approach cannot be generalized to other domains. For future component requests (20 days ahead), TacTex again employs additive regression to learn an adjustment between the current day's price and the future price (20 day ahead). Their algorithm is otherwise unchanged from the next day method.

Deep Maize uses a linear interpolation over recent samples to estimate the component price for a specific due date. An adjustment to the linear interpolation is computed from a reduced error pruning tree, a decision tree variant. The reduced error pruning tree offset values are trained offline using historical data of next day predictions. This same method is used for 20 day ahead predictions [4].

The CMieux agent uses a k-nearest neighbor approach to estimate next day component costs. The contribution of the k-nearest neighbors is averaged using inverse distance weighting, where distance refers to the temporal difference between the due date requests [5].

Multivariate Techniques. The literature contains several classes of methods that systematically leverage information from multiple related time series including vector autoregressive moving average (ARMA) and multivariate regression methods.

Vector ARMA is the multivariate analog of the ARMA time-series predictor presented in [8,9]. Vector ARMA is applied in [10] using the MISO TFN algorithm (Multiple Input Single Output Transfer Function-Noise model) to improve river flow predictions on a network of hydropower generating stations. Given daily flow data from three upstream and one downstream reservoirs, the authors developed an improved flow prediction model for both next-day and two day ahead predictions. The improvement was made using three years of daily flow measurements from all four sites and reduced standard error over the conventional approach of using separate time-series ARMA models for each site.

The vector ARMA also appears to be effective in domains with a small sample size. Disadvantages of vector ARMA stem from its sensitivity to collinearity in the input variables; the examples from the literature use only a small number (3-5) of input variables.

Multiple linear regression (MLR), principal component regression (PCR), and partial least squares (PLS) regression are techniques first used with significant success in chemometrics, social science, and econometrics [11]. PLS regression was particularly successful, compared to other methods, on problems having a large number of highly collinear variables and a small number of samples [12].

The behavior of PLS, MLR, and PCR regression techniques differ from the time-series based techniques due to the absence of a "memory" component. Time series models like ARMA can be affected by outliers in the input data, and the effect of an outlier can persist in the output prediction long after the outlier was first observed [13]. This is in contrast to the regression techniques: input observations that are outliers will only affect the output variable when the outlier is still in the input set. In adversarial settings like TAC SCM, where opponents have the ability to temporarily affect the input data to a prediction computation, the long term effect of outliers in time-series predictors is particularly undesirable.

3   Our Approach

The prediction model that PLS regression computes for a variable y is a weighted linear function in terms of the feature values x_i, $i = 1..m$ (where m is the number of features). Mathematically, the prediction model for a variable y can be expressed as[1]: $y = \hat{b}_0 + \hat{b}_1 x_1 + \hat{b}_2 x_2 + \ldots + \hat{b}_m x_m$ where $\hat{b}_i$, $i \in 0..m$ are the regression coefficients computed in the model calibration stage. This form of linear model is suitable for the economic modeling we are interested in and is discussed next.

3.1   A Simple Model

In an economic supply chain context, this simple linear model maps naturally into the domain: the long-run price of a product should be equivalent to a linear sum of the costs of its constituent parts plus the profit margin taken by the manufacturer. The cost of a component could similarly be computed from this ideal model: the long-run cost of some component should be equivalent to a fraction of the prices of products that use the component.

This ideal model, while intuitively attractive, is not sufficient for modeling prices in TAC SCM for several reasons. First, the model does not directly address lead time

---

[1] This is a parsimonious expression of the regression model. In practice, it may be useful to compute y values in a two step process employing, first, the dimensionality reduction and, second, the regression.

effects[2]. Also, particularly in the component market, prices vary significantly by lead time: longer lead time requests typically have lower cost. This mismatch between possible lead times in the two markets drives the need for agents to develop mechanisms for coordination, dynamic planning, and prediction. For this reason our model incorporates price observations for multiple component lead times.

Second, the model does not address trends that can be anticipated by observing changes in price over time. Observations of prices of an individual product over several past time steps $(p_t, p_{t-1}, p_{t-2}, \dots)$ provide information to form a prediction about the next product price (p_{t+1}). This is equivalent to a univariate time series prediction. Information from previous time steps is included in our model.

Third, visible non-price information about the environment also has an effect on prices. For instance, the current bank interest rate (the cost of borrowing), and the current storage cost (the cost of holding inventory) both affect price. They are also included in our model.

Fourth, information about the current market situation also has an effect on price. Information about overall aggregate demand is available to the agents by observing the number of products requested by customers each day. This information can also be included in the feature vector. In keeping with the domain-agnostic nature of our approach, we assume a linear relationship for the non-price features as well.

Including all observable information that could have an effect on price into the feature vector is an obvious approach. But in practice, this is impractical. First, as the number of features rises significantly, the effectiveness of the prediction algorithm is likely to degrade. Second, there is almost no limit to the number of possible features that can be added. The inclusion of irrelevant (or low informational value) features is a problem that we address next.

3.2   Input Feature Computation

We now illustrate how several distinct types of data are aggregated into a feature vector of consistent size. Data observable from an individual agent's perspective consists of four feature types:

1. *Game instance features* include values that remain invariant throughout the simulation instance, such as the bank interest rate and storage cost.
2. *Daily market segment demand* is computed from the total number of product Requests for Quotes (RFQs) in each of the three product market segments (low, medium, and high range) on each day.
3. *Daily price observations for products* are the mean sale prices for each of the 16 product types, as observed from the agent. Days with missing product price observations (no successful sales for a specific product on a given day) have their values

---

[2] In both the component and product markets, agents must commit to buy components or sell products far in advance of the delivery date. In the component market, delivery lead times can be between 1 and 220 days into the future. When an agent makes a component request, it must also specify the delivery date for the request. In the product market, delivery lead times are between 3 and 12 days into the future. The delivery date is specified in the request from the customer, and the agent with the winning bid must honor it or a significant financial per-unit late fee is imposed.

Table 1. List of all the features available to an agent during the TAC SCM competition

	Feature Type	Count	Feature
1	Game Instance	2	– storage cost – interest rate
2	Daily Demand	3	– low market – medium market – high market
3	Price for products	16	– SKU 1 ... – SKU 16
4	Price for parts at LT2$^\alpha$	16	– comp100sup1lt2$^\beta$ – comp101sup1lt2 – comp110sup2lt2 – comp111sup2lt2 ...
	Price for parts at LT6	16	– comp100sup1lt6 – comp101sup1lt6 ...
	Price for parts at LT10	16	...
	Price for parts at LT20	16	...
	Price for parts at LT30	16	...
	All Features	101	

$^\alpha$ LT2 denotes a delivery lead time of 2 days from the order date.
$^\beta$ Price of component 100 from supplier 1 with a delivery lead-time of 2 days.

computed using a radial basis function interpolation. No consideration is made for variations in lead-time among product price observations.

4. *Daily price observations for components* are the prices of each of the 10 unique components, as observed by the agent. There are 16 product lines for the 10 components, often with significant price difference for the components produced by more than one line. The prices are added to the feature vector for a pre-defined schedule of lead times of 2, 6, 10, 20, and 30 days. Because we use 5 lead times, each component contributes 5 features to the overall feature set. Days with missing component observations on these lead times have their values computed using a radial basis function interpolation over observations for the component from the previous 5 days.

These input features combine to produce a vector of 101 features (see Table 1). A feature vector of the complete feature set can be computed for each day for each agent perspective in a simulation run. The feature vectors can be computed sequentially in ascending time unit order from day 1 to 219. The features for each type can be computed based on messages visible to an individual agent (in the case of these experiments, the prediction challenge agent's perspective is used). For a day when there are no observed values for a particular component and lead-time (the agent did not request any of a particular component, for example), the value for that day is computed using radial basis function interpolation of data available to the agent on that day (including data from previous days). For days at the beginning of a simulation (when no past observations are available), a lookup table of price statistics from the beginning of all training set simulations is used to bootstrap the feature vector.

Labeled training instances are generated by computing the matrix of observations for the features and appending the known true value (label) for the regression target. The true value is the actual median unit price for each game, time unit, product, and lead time combination. This labeled training set is read by the PLS algorithm to produce a regression model.

Table 2. A simple configuration for product prediction. A "•" denotes inclusion of a particular feature class having the specified time lag.

Class	Lagged Offsets					
	0	1	2	4	8	16
P3	•					
P3b	•					
P3c	•					
P2	•					
P4	•					
P4h	•					

3.3   Lagged Features and Hierarchical Segmentation

Using only the most recent values of the 101 possible features as the entire feature set may provide reasonable prediction results in some domains, but, it cannot predict trends or temporal relationships present in the data. The need to represent temporally-offset relationships motivates the idea of adding time-delayed observations to the feature set as well; we refer to this as the addition of *lagged features*. For instance, if it is known that the cost of a component on day $t - 8$ is most representative of the price of a product sold on day $t + 1$, the 8 day delayed observation of that component should have a high weight in the model. The time delay could correspond to the delay between persistent changes in the observations and the resulting effect in the mean agent behavior.

Our technique uses the assumption that more recent observations are likely to have high informational value for price prediction, but time-delayed features may hold informational value as well (i.e. the environment is not completely stochastic). The reason for valuing recent observation more is that customer demand in each market segment follows a Poisson distribution with a random walk. The lead time between a change in the market and its effect on other prices may be longer than one day, but the minimum possible lead time for this effect is 1 day. To cover the possibility of changes in the design of opponent agents outside of our control, we keep most recent (current day) observations in the model. For reasons of tractability, features with long time delays are only added after features with shorter delays are added. Even with this constraint, searching for the optimal subset from 101 available features is still an intractably large search space.

To reduce the number of possible configurations of features, we introduce the notion of a hierarchical segmentation of the feature set. In this domain, each of the 101 features is placed into one of several classes based on its relationship to the target variable. In cases where a feature belongs to multiple classes, the feature is placed in the class that is most specific. From a minimal amount of domain knowledge derived from the specification document of TAC SCM, we have compiled a class hierarchy for each type of target variable. These hierarchies can be seen for the product prediction and component prediction tasks in Figures 1 and 2, respectively.

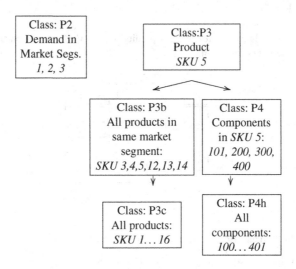

Fig. 1. Lag scheme class hierarchy for product price prediction. Arrow denotes a *not greater than* relationship (i.e. class P4 should have an equal or lower maximum time offset than class P3).

Thus far we have explained how a better feature set can be chosen based on some knowledge of the domain. Now we will address how to choose the time-delayed data from each class. The simplest lag configuration, shown in Table 2, contains the most recent day's value from all feature classes. We posit that time-delayed observations from the variable of interest (*Class P3*) are likely to be predictive as well. Time-delayed observations from other feature classes *may also be* but are less likely to be predictive. This is the principle on which the choice of hierarchy and strict ordering of lagged data additions is based.

We need to chose the set of permitted lagged offsets from each class. In this domain, we have found two sets of time-delays to be useful: time-delays with integer offsets $\{\varnothing^3, 0, 1, 2, 3, 4, 5, \ldots\}$ and time-delays with geometrically increasing offsets $\{\varnothing, 0, 1, 2, 4, 8, 16, \ldots\}$.

As as example, let's consider product SKU 5. In Figure 1, the earlier observations of the variable to be predicted (*Class P3*) are most likely to contain predictive information. Information about other similar products (*Class P4*) will also provide some information (but likely are less informationally dense). Finally, information about all other products is expected to contain the least information density (*Class P4h*). By constraining

---

[3] This symbol refers to the lack of any observation.

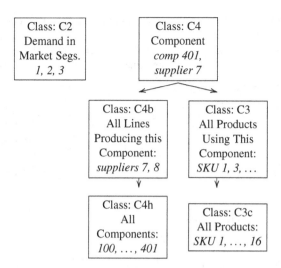

Fig. 2. Lag scheme class hierarchy for component prediction

the classes so that the less informationally dense classes have lower time delays and contribute fewer additional features, we prevent the inclusion of extraneous, irrelevant features.

Next, we will show how the time lagged data is constructed to form the augmented features set. An expansion of the feature set is referred to as a *lag scheme expansion*. Of course, the optimal lag scheme may be different for each variable modeled; a search of the possible configurations is performed to find the best performing configuration in each prediction class.

The number of possible lag schemes as formulated with the hierarchies in Figures 1 and 2 for a maximum time delay of 16 days are 11172^4 for both products and components. Without the constraints between classes, there are 117649 configurations[5] of the 6 feature classes if constrained to possible time delays of $\{\varnothing, 0, 1, 2, 4, 8, 16\}$, but many of these configurations are uninteresting variants. Finally, without the hierarchical segmentation and constraints between classes, there are 7^{101} ($\approx 10^{85}$) configurations of the 101 original features. Thus imposing both the feature classification and the constraint hierarchy allows for a greater range of "interesting" lag schemes to be tested for the same amount of lag scheme search.

The optimal lag schemes we use in our experimental results in each of the four prediction classes are provided in Table 3. For instance, the current product prediction shown in Table 3(a) uses 35 raw features that are expanded into 56 augmented features. Feature classes contributing features are: P3 (1 raw feature $\times$ 10 discrete lags), P3b (5

---

[4] This is the subset of the 117649 configurations where all constraints between classes are satisfied. For example, if in a specific configuration class P2 contains time delays $\{0, 1, 2\}$ it would not be permissible for P3 to have time delays $\{0, 1, 2, 4\}$. All configurations with this set of values would be discarded from the set of possible lag configurations.

[5] There are 7 possible configurations of each class, and there are 6 classes. Therefore, there are $7^6 = 117649$ possible configurations.

Table 3. Optimal lag schemes for the four prediction classes. Each prediction class was searched independently to find the optimal lag scheme. There are 57 augmented features for current product prediction, 51 for future product prediction, 10 for current component prediction, and 102 for future component prediction. A "•" indicates time lags for feature classes that are included.

Class	Lagged Offsets									
	0	1	2	3	4	5	6	7	8	9
P3	•	•	•	•	•	•	•	•	•	•
P3b	•									
P3c	•									
P2	•	•	•	•	•					
P4	•									
P4h	•									

(a) current product prediction

Class	Lagged Offsets					
	0	1	2	4	8	16
P3	•	•	•	•	•	
P3b	•	•	•	•	•	
P3c						
P2	•	•	•	•	•	
P4	•					
P4h						

(b) future product prediction

Class	Lagged Offsets									
	0	1	2	3	4	5	6	7	8	9
C4	•	•	•	•	•	•	•	•		
C4b										
C4h										
C3										
C3c										
C2										

(c) current component prediction

Class	Lagged Offsets					
	0	1	2	4	8	16
C4	•	•	•	•	•	
C4b						
C4h						
C3	•	•	•	•	•	
C3c						
C2	•	•	•	•	•	

(d) future component prediction

raw features (P3 contains the 6th feature) × 1 discrete lag), P3c (10 raw features (P3 and P3b handle 6 of the 16 SKUs) × 1 discrete lag), P2 (3 raw features × 5 discrete lags), P4 (7 raw features × 1 discrete lag), P4h (9 raw features × 1 discrete lag), and two game invariant features (game storage cost, game interest rate). While a domain expert could conceive of a generally high-performance feature set, the automated lag scheme search produces a configuration similar to what a domain expert could build without the cost of requiring a domain expert. Also, the results of the optimal lag scheme search can elicit some surprising relationships found in the data.

3.4   Partial Least Squares Regression

The methodology presented here does not modify the PLS algorithm, so our treatment of PLS is brief. Several implementations of PLS exist [14,15,11]; each with its own performance characteristics. This work uses the orthogonalized PLS, Non-Integer Partial Least Squares (NIPALS), implementation presented in [12]. PLS was chosen over similar multivariate techniques including multiple linear regression, ridge regression [16], and principal component regression [17] because it produces generally equivalent or better performance than the others and has the ability to adjust model complexity. Specific advantages of this algorithm are presented.

Partial least squares regression is particularly applicable to modeling economic phenomena. First, PLS regression is able to handle very high-dimensionality inputs because

---

Algorithm 1. PLS1 Calibration

---

        input : A matrix X containing n training samples, n rows each with m features.
               The corresponding vector y containing n labels for the training set. Model
               complexity A_{max} chosen so that $a = 1, \ldots, A_{max}$.
        output: Loading arrays $\hat{W}$, $\hat{Q}$, and $\hat{P}$.

STEP 1 $X_0 = X - 1\bar{x}'$, where $\bar{x}'$ is a vector of the
             mean values of the variables in X.
             $y_0 = y - 1\bar{y}$, where $\bar{y}$ is the mean value of y

optional Normalize columns in X_0 to have equivalent variance. (Divide each column by
             its variance.)

        for $a = 1 \rightarrow A_{max}$ **do**

STEP 2.1   Using least squares, compute normalized local model $\hat{w}_a$
             $\hat{w}_a = X'_{a-1} y_{a-1} / \| X'_{a-1} y_{a-1} \|$

STEP 2.2   Estimate scores $\hat{t}_a$ using model $\hat{w}_a$.
             $\hat{t}_a = X_{a-1} \hat{w}_a$ (since $\hat{w}'_a \hat{w}_a = 1$)

STEP 2.3   Estimate x-loadings p_a using scores $\hat{t}_a$.
             $\hat{p}'_a = X'_{a-1} \hat{t}_a / \hat{t}'_a \hat{t}_a$

STEP 2.4   Estimate y-loadings q_a using scores $\hat{t}_a$.
             $y_{a-1} = \hat{t}_a q_a + f$
             $\hat{q}_a = y'_{a-1} \hat{t}_a / \hat{t}'_a \hat{t}_a$

STEP 2.5   Update X and y with contribution of current a.
             $X_a = X_{a-1} - \hat{t}_a \hat{p}'_a$
             $y_a = y_{a-1} - \hat{t}_a \hat{q}_a$

        end

---

it implicitly performs dimensionality reduction from the number of inputs to the number of PLS factors. Second, the model complexity can be adjusted by changing the number of PLS factors to use in computing the regression result. This value is adjusted in our experiments to determine the optimal model complexity in each prediction class. Third, the algorithm is generally robust to the inclusion of highly collinear or irrelevant features. Fourth, the structure of a trained model can be examined for knowledge about the domain.

Mathematically, PLS regression deterministically computes a linear function that maps a vector of the input features x_i into the output variable y_i (the label). Using a PLS regression model for a particular variable y requires a calibration to be performed over a set of training samples to determine the model as computed using Algorithm 1.

The model can be used for prediction as described mathematically in Algorithm 2.

4 Model Parameter: Dimensionality Reduction

The PLS regression algorithm in [12] allows users to adjust the model complexity by selecting the number of PLS factors to generate when training. (These factors are analogous to the principal component vectors used in principal component regression.) The number of PLS factors determines the dimensionality of the intermediate variable space

---

Algorithm 2. PLS1 Prediction

---

input : Populated feature vector $\mathbf{x}_i$, calibration $\bar{x}$, calibration $\bar{y}$, loading weights $\hat{W}$, loadings $\hat{P}$, loadings $\hat{Q}$, (for optional step) matrix X containing n training samples (denoted as row vectors $\mathbf{x}_i$)

output: Prediction of $\hat{y}_i$

STEP 1 Center observation of feature vector x_i.
$$x_{i,0} = x_i - 1\bar{x}'$$

optional Normalize variance $x'_{i,0}$ by dividing each value by its column variance in calibration X.

for $a = 1 \rightarrow A_{max}$ **do**

STEP 2.1 | Compute contribution of $\hat{w}_a$ to y_i.
$$\hat{t}_{i,a} = x'_{i,a} - 1\hat{w}_a$$
$$x_{i,a} = x_{i,a-1} - \hat{t}_{i,a}\hat{p}'_a$$

end

STEP 3 Compute prediction of y_i
$$\hat{y}_i = \bar{y} + \Sigma_{a=1}^A \hat{t}_{i,a}\hat{q}_a$$

Alt. Alternative formulation in 1 step using $\hat{b}$.
$$\hat{b}_0 = \bar{y} - \bar{x}'\hat{b}$$
$$\hat{B} = \hat{W}(\hat{P}'\hat{W})^{-1}\hat{Q}$$
$$\hat{y}_i = 1\hat{b}_0 + x'_i\hat{B}$$

---

that the data is mapped to. The computational complexity does not significantly increase for a larger number of factors but the choice does have an effect on prediction performance: too large a number can cause over-fitting, and too small a number can cause the model to be unable to represent the relationships in the data. We varied the number of factors systematically in the optimal lag scheme search. The best performing number of components is shown for each prediction category in Section 5.

When computing the optimal lag scheme it is also critical to determine the correct value for model complexity in PLS. Figure 3 shows how the prediction accuracy varies based on model complexity relative to the best observed prediction error (the lag scheme is not varied in the data in this graph). The future component class has a slightly different pattern: we conjecture that future component achieves optimal error with a lower number of latent variables because it has a relatively larger number of inputs from the lag scheme search. Empirical results show that it is generally better to err on the side of excess model complexity but excess complexity can also reduce prediction accuracy by, in one case, over 10% above the lowest achievable error.

5   Experimental Results

We evaluate our approach on the TAC SCM 2008 Prediction challenge data set consisting of 48 experimental runs divided into 3 sets of 16 games. Each set has a different mixture of agents. The games were divided using a standard 6-fold cross validation for training and scoring. For example, the first fold consisted of a training set of games 9-16 in set A and all games from sets B and C, and a test set of games 1-8 in set A.

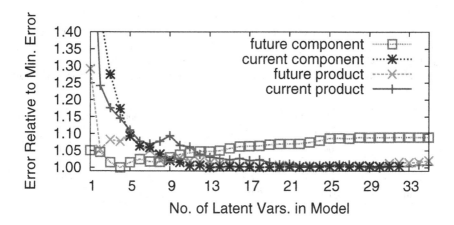

Fig. 3. Effect of varying the model complexity (number of PLS factors) for the optimal lag scheme. The number of factors used in our experiments varied by prediction class: (1) current product used 18 factors, (2) future product used 22 factors, (3) current component used 22 factors, and (4) future component used 4 factors. The listed number of features used for each prediction class is found by searching the range of possible values (between 1 and the number of features).

In order to compute prices for all variables in each prediction class, one prediction model is generated for each variable to predict. The number of prediction models by class is:

1. 16 for current product prices (one for each product type),
2. 16 for future product prices,
3. 16×59 for current component prices (one for each component line-lead time pair for lead times 2 to 60), and
4. 16×26 for future component prices (lead times 5 to 30)

The lag scheme used for each prediction class was computed using an exhaustive search over all lag schemes with valid hierarchical relationships on folds 1, 3, and 5 of the 6-fold cross validation set.

The results shown in Table 4 are the aggregate scores obtained from experiments on the entire 6-fold set using the best performing lag schemes. The results show that incorporating time-delayed features onto the prediction task does improve the overall prediction accuracy when compared with no use of lagged data. A comparison with the published results shows that our method is competitive against state-of-the-art methods used within the top performing agents. In particular, our method outperforms existing methods on 20 day ahead predictions in both the component market and the product market. The prediction category for which our method does worst ("current product") can be explained by the fact that the regression model computes a point estimate for sales of each product on each day and uses the same price for all queries of the same product on a specific day. There may be some attribute in product requests that causes prices to vary significantly among the set of requests for the same product on the same

Table 4. Comparison between the error scores of an agent implementing our method for each of the 4 classes of prediction and the scores of the top performing agents in the 2008 Prediction Challenge. The Student's t-test p-value when compared against 2008 First Place agent for Future Product of PLS with geom. lag is 0.2660, for Future Component is 0.0012. A p-value (p-val) of less than 0.05 indicates that the results of the two algorithms being compared are statistically different at the 95% confidence level.

RMSE	Current Product	Future Product	Current Component	Future Component
PLS (geom. lag)	0.06308	**0.08553**	0.04063	**0.09910**
PLS (int. lags)	0.06295	0.09264	0.04008	0.10020
PLS (no lag)	0.06300	0.09039	0.04468	0.10947
2008 First Place	0.04779	0.08726	0.03476	0.09964
2008 Third Place	0.0531	0.09934	0.04029	0.10281

day. For "future product", a point estimate is sufficient because the true value represents the median price for product sales 20 days ahead.

The optimal lag schemes used in each of the four prediction classes is provided in Table 3. There are some feature classes that are not included at all in the optimal lag scheme, an example of this appears in Table 3(c): data from class C4 are the only lagged features used in the prediction model. This suggests that the other variables are not significant to the prediction of current component prices.

6   Conclusions and Future Work

Prediction problems that are dynamic and possess high dimensionality are generally difficult to model well. It is easy to disregard predictive information sources in exchange for model simplicity. Imposing a class-based feature hierarchy and using time-delayed data extraction in conjunction with a multivariate regression approach provides a modeling framework that maximizes the use of available predictive inputs while being robust to irrelevant data. Hierarchical classification of features is of benefit because it reduces the search space for finding the best lag configurations.

We believe that the time-delayed data extraction and classification is not tied to PLS Regression for good performance. But, PLS regression was chosen because of its desirable properties for high-dimensional domains. In applications where performance is a significant consideration, it may be possible to compute the regression results for several target variables simultaneously in a single model PLS model using a variant called PLS2 regression. Also, the mathematical description of the trained regression model itself can be leveraged to develop domain knowledge about relationships between variables in the domain. More opaque, "black box" machine learning models may not facilitate this. There are several aspects of PLS regression that could be explored to refine and expand on these results. First, in prediction mode, PLS regression can also measure prediction confidence on each observation by analysis of the residuals computed in the regression. Another direction of future research is related to analysis of the loading vectors of the PLS model to attempt to compute causal relationships between lagged variables. Additionally, this information could be used for manual validation of the computed models.

Also, this analysis may facilitate better decision making in the application domain. In TAC SCM, empirically constructed causal models may allow agent developers to focus on specific behaviors that affect prices.

We believe this approach is highly applicable to other economic data sets. In particular, this data preparation and prediction method may have application in cases where there are significant spatial relationships between input sources. Examples of such domains include airline ticket pricing and river-flow prediction. This is an area left for future work.

References

1. Collins, J., Arunachalam, R., Sadeh, N., Ericsson, J., Finne, N., Janson, S.: The Supply Chain Management Game for the 2006 Trading Agent Competition. Technical Report CMU-ISRI-07-100, Carnegie Mellon University, Pittsburgh, PA (December 2006)
2. Pardoe, D., Stone, P.: The 2007 TAC SCM Prediction Challenge. In: Ketter, W., La Poutré, H., Sadeh, N., Shehory, O., Walsh, W. (eds.) AMEC 2008. LNBIP, vol. 44, pp. 175–189. Springer, Heidelberg (2010)
3. Pardoe, D., Stone, P.: An Autonomous Agent for Supply Chain Management. In: Adomavicius, G., Gupta, A. (eds.) Handbooks in Information Systems Series: Business Computing. Elsevier (2007)
4. Kiekintveld, C., Miller, J., Jordan, P.R., Callender, L.F., Wellman, M.P.: Forecasting Market Prices in a Supply Chain Game. Electronic Commerce Research and Applications 8(2), 63–77 (2009)
5. Benisch, M., Sardinha, A., Andrews, J., Ravichandran, R., Sadeh, N.: CMieux: Adaptive Strategies for Competitive Supply Chain Trading. Electronic Commerce Research and Applications 8(2), 78–90 (2009)
6. Collins, J., Ketter, W., Gini, M.: Flexible Decision Control in an Autonomous Trading Agent. Electronic Commerce Research and Applications 8(2), 91–105 (2009)
7. Ketter, W., Collins, J., Gini, M., Gupta, A., Schrater, P.: Detecting and Forecasting Economic Regimes in Multi-Agent Automated Exchanges. Decision Support Systems 47(4), 307–318 (2009)
8. Box, G., Pelham, E., Jenkins, G.M.: Time Series Analysis: Forecasting and Control, 3rd edn. Prentice Hall PTR (1994)
9. Tiao, G.C., Box, G.E.P.: Modeling Multiple Time Series with Applications. Journal of the American Statistical Association 76(376), 802–816 (1981)
10. Olason, T., Watt, W.E.: Multivariate Transfer Function-Noise Model of River Flow for Hydropower Operation. Nordic Hydrology 17(3), 185–202 (1986)
11. Martens, H., Næs, T.: Multivariate Calibration. John Wiley & Sons (July 1992)
12. Wold, S., Martens, H., Wold, H.: The multivariate calibration problem in chemistry solved by the PLS method. In: Matrix Pencils. LNM, vol. 973, pp. 286–293. Springer (1983)
13. Hillmer, S.C., Larcker, D.F., Schroeder, D.A.: Forecasting Accounting Data: A Multiple Time-Series Analysis. Journal of Forecasting 2(4), 389–404 (1983)
14. de Jong, S.: SIMPLS: An Alternative Approach to Partial Least Squares Regression. Chemometrics and Intelligent Laboratory Systems 18(3), 251–263 (1993)
15. Dayal, B.S., MacGregor, J.F.: Recursive Exponentially Weighted PLS and its Applications to Adaptive Control and Prediction. Journal of Process Control 7(3), 169–179 (1997)
16. Hoerl, A.E., Kennard, R.W.: Ridge Regression: Biased Estimation for Nonorthogonal Problems. Technometrics 42(1), 80–86 (2000)
17. Jolliffe, I.T.: A Note on the Use of Principal Components in Regression. Journal of Royal Statistical Society (Applied Statistics) 31(3), 300–303 (1982)

Testing Adaptive Expectations Models of a Continuous Double Auction Market against Empirical Facts

Neil Rayner[1], Steve Phelps[1], and Nick Constantinou[2]

[1] Center for Computational Finance and Economic Agents (CCFEA), University of Essex,
Colchester, CO4 3SQ, United Kingdom
njwray@essex.ac.uk
[2] Essex Business School, University of Essex, Colchester, CO4 3SQ, United Kingdom

Abstract. It is well known that empirical financial time series data exhibit long memory phenomena: the behaviour of the market at various times in the past continues to exert an influence in the present. One explanation for these phenomena is that they result from a process of social learning in which poorly performing agents switch their strategy to that of other agents who appear to be more successful. We test this explanation using an agent-based model and we find that the stability of the model is directly related to the dynamics of the learning process; models in which learning converges to a stationary steady state fail to produce realistic time series data. In contrast, models in which learning leads to *dynamic* switching behaviour in the steady state are able to reproduce the long memory phenomena. We demonstrate that a model which incorporates contrarian trading strategies results in more dynamic behaviour in steady state, and hence is able to produce more realistic results.

Keywords: agent-based models, adaptive expectations, market microstructure, long memory.

1 Introduction

With the explosion of algorithmic trading, financial markets now constitute some of the largest and most mission critical multi-agent systems in our society. Understanding the behaviour of these markets would make an important contribution to the prevention of future financial crises. There is a need to build models of *actual* electronic markets, and to validate these models against empirical facts – that is, to attempt to *reverse engineer* existing multi-agent systems in order to understand how they work. Such an exercise is now possible with the availability of electronic data detailing every transaction in the market which can run to gigabytes per year per financial asset, and can be purchased from the major financial exchanges by any third party. Towards this end we introduce an agent-based model which produces behaviour consistent with several phenomena that have been widely documented from studies of empirical financial data. Our model is in the tradition of *adaptive expectations* [5] models in which: (i) agents' valuations are determined by their expectations of what will happen in the market in the *future*, for example their belief that the market price will rise or fall; and (ii) expectations are formed inductively through a learning process, rather than through the framework of rational expectations. This type of model is in contrast to auction theoretic models which

E. David et al. (Eds.): AMEC/TADA 2011, LNBIP 119, pp. 44–56, 2013.

typically assume that valuations are private information, are well defined, uncorrelated, or do not change over time, or some combination of these. In contrast the adaptive expectations framework proposes a much more dynamic view of agents' beliefs as they constantly revise their expectations, and hence valuations, in response to observations of other agents and the market itself: the market is an "expectations feedback system" from which valuations emerge [6].

The focus of our analysis is to determine to what extent this picture of the market is consistent with the empirical data from real exchanges. Initially we examine properties which are observable in empirical high frequency trading data with a view to model validation. Once our model is validated, we can use it to answer counter factual questions such as how changes in the design of the market mechanism would affect the efficiency of the market. Therefore we focus on well known "stylized facts" of high-frequency time series data observed in real financial markets and we analyse to what extent different model assumptions are consistent with these phenomena. Specifically we analyze long memory in the following attributes:

1. *Volume*: Over periods of time volume can be consistently high or low [12];
2. *Volatility*: Periods of similar volatility (price fluctuations) are observed [3,4,7,14,13,15];
3. *Order Signs*: Signs of orders (that is, buy orders have a positive sign and sell orders have a negative sign) exhibit long memory [10]; and
4. *Returns*: Returns do not exhibit long memory [1]. (Similar returns do not cluster together in time).

In Section 2 we describe an existing agent-based model [8,9] within which agents learn trading strategies from each other. These landmark experiments demonstrated the power of agent-based modelling and specifically its ability to address poorly understood phenomena like long memory in high frequency financial data. We extend this model by introducing more contrarian forecasting strategies and demonstrate that this leads to an improvement in the robustness of the model. We validate the existing LeBaron and Yamamoto model in Section 3 and present our results in Section 4. In Section 5 we compare the ability of the LeBaron and Yamamoto model and our more contrarian model to produce long memory "stylized facts" of financial markets. Finally in Section 6 we conclude.

2   The Model

We attempt to explain the long memory phenomena using an adaptive expectations model with three classes of strategy which are used to form expectations about future returns:

1. *fundamentalists* value a stock through an understanding of its hypothetical underlying value, in other words, based on expectations of the long term profitability of the issuing company;
2. *chartists* form valuations inductively from historical price data; and

3. *noise traders* who trade based on the fluctuations of the price of a stock. The buying and selling behaviour of traders for a particular stock generates characteristic fluctuations in price. A stock has an emergent volatility, understanding this volatility allows traders to identify when the price is relatively low and when it is relatively high.

Although chartist strategies should not be profitable according to the efficient markets hypothesis, this is not necessarily true if the market is outside of an efficient equilibrium. For example, if many agents adopt a chartist forecasting strategy it may be rational to follow suit as the chartist expectations may lead to a self-fulfilling prophecy in the form of a speculative bubble. Thus there are feedback effects from these three classes of forecasting strategy and it is important to study the interaction between them in order to understand the macroscopic behaviour of the market as a whole.

We model the market mechanism as a continuous double auction with limit orders. Each agent submits a limit order to the market on every round of trading. Orders are executed using a time priority rule: the transaction price is the price of the order which was submitted first regardless of whether it is a bid or ask. If an order cannot be executed immediately it is queued on the order-book.

The sign (buy or sell) and the price of the order for agent i at time t is determined as a function of each agent's *forecast* of expected return $\hat{r}_{(i,t,t+\tau)}$ for the period $t + \tau$ (τ a constant defining the time horizon over which price expectations are made). The price of the order is set according to:

$$p_{(i,t+\tau)} = p_t \cdot e^{\hat{r}_{(i,t,t+\tau)}}$$

where p_t is the market quoted price at time t, and the sign of the order is buy iff. $p_{(i,t+\tau)} \geq p_t$ or sell iff. $p_{(i,t+\tau)} < p_t$.

In [8,9] the forecasted expected return for the period $t+\tau$ of agent i at time t is calculated with a linear combination of fundamentalist, chartist and noise-trader forecasting rules:

$$\hat{r}_{(i,t,t+\tau)} = \hat{r}_{f(i,t,t+\tau)} + \hat{r}_{c(i,t,t+\tau)} + \hat{r}_{n(i,t,t+\tau)} \tag{1}$$

$$\hat{r}_{f(i,t,t+\tau)} = f_{(i,t)} \cdot \left(\frac{F - p_t}{p_t}\right) \tag{2}$$

$$\hat{r}_{c(i,t,t+\tau)} = c_{(i,t)} \cdot \hat{r}_{L_i} \tag{3}$$

$$\hat{r}_{n(i,t,t+\tau)} = n_{(i,t)} \cdot \epsilon_{(i,t)} \tag{4}$$

In the above F is the so-called "fundamental price" (which is exogenous and fixed for all agents), p_t is the current market quoted price which is the value of the transaction at the previous time step or in the absence of a transaction the midpoint of the spread, $\epsilon_{(i,t)}$ are random iid. variables distributed $\sim N(0, 1)$ and $\hat{r}_{L_i}$ is a forecast based on historical data; in our case a moving average of actual market returns over the period L_i:

$$\hat{r}_{L_i} = \frac{1}{L_i} \sum_{j=1}^{L_i} \frac{p_{t-j} - p_{t-j-1}}{p_{t-j-1}}$$

The period L_i is randomly and uniformly initialised from the interval $(1, l_{max})$. The linear coefficients $f_{(i,t)}$, $c_{(i,t)}$ and $n_{(i,t)}$ denote the weight that agent i gives to each class of forecast amongst fundamentalist, chartist and noise-trader respectively at time t. Bids (b_t^i) and asks (a_t^i) (that is buys and sells) are entered into the with a markup or markdown.

$$b_t^i = p_{t,t+\tau}^i (1 - k^i) \tag{5}$$
$$a_t^i = p_{t,t+\tau}^i (1 + k^i) \tag{6}$$

k^i is randomly and uniformly initialised from an interval $(0, k_{max})$.

1. If a bid exceeds the best ask (lowest ask price on the order book) it is entered at the ask price (converted into a market order rather than a limit order).
2. If an ask is lower than the best bid (highest bid price on the order book) it is entered at the bid price (converted into a market order rather than a limit order).

Each agent enters the market with a constant probability λ. All orders have a limited order life, after which they are removed from the order book should they have not been successfully matched (a constant exogenously set to 200 units of time).

2.1 Learning

As in [8,9], agents use a co-evolutionary Genetic Algorithm to learn the coefficients $f_{(i,t)}$, $c_{(i,t)}$ and $n_{(i,t)}$. Each agent records its own forecast error as the market progresses and generates a fitness score s_i over a period of 5000 units of time. Each unit of time corresponds to the entry of an order into the market by an agent. Each agent presents 5 orders to the market in this period (the number of agents in these models being 1000).

$$s_i = \frac{1}{\sum_{t=1}^{5000} (p_t - p_{(i,t+\tau)})^2} \tag{7}$$

After 5000 units of time each combination of weights held by the agents is assigned a relative fitness score (S_i) normalised with respect to the population fitness.

$$S_i = \frac{s_i}{\sum_i s_i} \tag{8}$$

The strategy weights are copied by the learning agents in proportion to this score.

The *initial* values at time $t = 0$ for the fundamentalist $f_{(i,0)}$, chartist $c_{(i,0)}$ and noise $n_{(i,0)}$ weights are drawn from the following distributions:

$$f_{(i,0)} \sim |N(0, \sigma_f)|, \; c_{(i,0)} \sim N(0, \sigma_c), \; n_{(i,0)} \sim |N(0, \sigma_n)| \tag{9}$$

In addition to the learning of weights after each 5000 units of time, agents also may mutate one of their weights drawing a weight at random from the distributions in Equation 9.

We analyse two variants of this basic model; an existing model in the literature [8,9] in which forecasting strategies are linear *combinations* as per Equation 1 (henceforth we refer to this model as the LY model), and our own model in which each agent adopts either an *atomic* fundamentalist (Equation 2) , chartist (Equation 3) or noise trader (Equation 4) forecasting rule and not a linear combination as in the LY model above (Equation 1). Both our model and the LY model occupy the same strategy space. However, in our model, two out of the three weights are zero reducing each agent to just one of the return forecast rules (Equation 2, Equation 3 or Equation 4).

In [2] two main types of strategy are identified; momentum strategies based on the following of trends, and contrarian strategies based on the reversal of trends. Contrarian traders predict price reversals and make profit (when they are correct) by positioning themselves to take advantage of that reversal. These two diametrically opposed strategies appear to exist simultaneously [2]. For example, in a rising trend momentum strategists will place bid orders (buys) in the market while contrarian strategists will place asks orders (sells). Other factors contribute to contrarian like behaviour. For example,"pairs trading" where a pair of related stocks are traded together such that when one is relatively expensive and the other cheap, traders sell the expensive one and buy the cheap one which can be a behaviour which is entirely independent of the current trends in the market. Other contrarian-like behaviours can be caused by events external to the market, for example arbitrage opportunities; prices for the same stock can differ between two markets so traders buy in the cheaper market and sell in the more expensive market (gaining risk-free profit). This arbitrage behaviour can be counter to the trends in the market.

The LY Model implements contrarianism by allowing the chartist weight to go negative (Equation 9). In the LY Model agents imitate successful strategies: if the most successful strategy employs a negative chartist weight then agents will tend to adopt that strategy. The negative chartist weight would then represent not a contrarian position but the strategy of the momentum strategists. Contrarian strategists seek to behave in a contrary way to the momentum strategists. To capture this behaviour we introduce additional contrarianism. We add two contrarian strategies; one is to negate the learned trend, so the contrarian agent predicts a price move in the opposite direction of the learned trend (e.g if the learned chartist trend is negative then the contrarians will predict a price move in a positive direction and vice versa), and the second to zero the trend predicting that the price will not trend in the learnt direction at all but will remain at its current level. We have chosen to implement this firstly by setting the contrarian chartist strategy to the negative of the non-contrarian chartist strategy:

$$\hat{r}_{c_c(i,t,t+\tau)} = -\hat{r}_{c(i,t,t+\tau)}$$

Secondly we set the contrarian fundamentalist and noise strategies to be the zeroed non-contrarian fundamentalist and noise strategies:

$$\hat{r}_{f_c(i,t,t+\tau)} = \hat{r}_{n_c(i,t,t+\tau)} = 0$$

In the *contrarian* variant agents can choose from the following discrete set of return forecasting strategies:

$$\{\hat{r}_{c(i,t,t+\tau)}, \hat{r}_{f(i,t,t+\tau)}, \hat{r}_{n(i,t,t+\tau)},$$
$$\hat{r}_{f_c(i,t,t+\tau)}, \hat{r}_{n_c(i,t,t+\tau)}, \hat{r}_{c_c(i,t,t+\tau)}\}$$

The same learning process operates in this model as in the LY model (but with the addition of the contrarian parameter). So an agent can change from fundamentalist to chartist or contrarian to non-contrarian to take advantage of a better strategy. During initialisation of the model values are drawn randomly from the distributions in Equation 9 as in the LY model, but each agent also chooses randomly between being a fundamentalist, chartist or noise trader and contrarian or non-contrarian. Henceforth we refer to this latter model as "the Contrarian Model".

3 Methodology and Model Validation

We compare model assumptions according to how well a particular model reproduces the long-memory phenomena. To compare models we test their long-memory properties using Lo's modified rescaled range (R/S) statistic [11] (sometimes called range over standard deviation). The statistic is designed to compare the maximum and minimum values of running sums of deviations from the sample mean, re-normalized by the

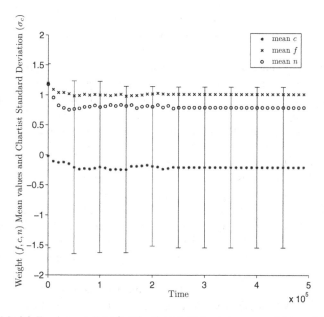

Fig. 1. LY Model. Fundamentalist (f), Chartist (c), Noise (n) mean weights and Chartist Standard Deviation (σ_c) with time

sample standard deviation. The deviations are greater in the presence of long-memory than in the absence of long-memory. The Lo R/S statistic includes the weighted auto-covariance up to lag q to capture the effects of short-range dependence.

Our first experiment tests the conjecture that imitation (in the LY Model) is sufficient to produce the long memory phenomena by attempting to reject the null hypothesis that long memory is caused by the strategies that each agent adopts and not by learning at all. The model is simulated in two sequential phases with different treatment factors:

1. a learning phase in which the agent's genetic algorithm searches for strategies with high relative fitness (see Equation 7 and Equation 8).
2. a commitment phase where agent's commit to a learned strategy and perform no further learning.

The default experiment time is 250000 time units (taken from [8,9]). The experiment has been executed for twice the default experiment time (2 x 250000 units of time); the learning phase is executed for half the experiment time (the default time) and then the commitment phase is started and runs for the same period. Default parameter values are displayed in Table 1 these values have been taken from [8,9] except the standard deviations of the weight distributions which are all set to 1.5 and the probability of entering the market which is set to 1.0. These values are all varied in our tests on model stability.

4   Validation Results for LY Model

In Figure 1 we show the mean value (across all agents) of the fundamentalist (f), chartist (c) and the noise trader weight (n) with respect to time. It also shows the chartist weight distribution standard deviation (σ_c) (the noise and fundamentalist weight distribution standard deviation are not shown but behave in a similar manner). As we can see in Figure 1 the agents move initially very quickly to a region in the strategy space. There is then a period of mean fluctuation as the agents move about in that region (not converging to any specific strategy). When the commitment phase starts and the agents stick with the strategy they have found, movement in the weights cease and we end up with a straight line for the mean value of the weights over the remainder of the experiment time with no change in the weight distribution standard deviations.Results are shown in tables which present the percentage of executions exhibiting long memory in volume, volatility, signs of orders (buy or sell orders) and returns for each experiment. The experiment was executed 100 times; the results are summarised in Tables 2 and 3. In the first phase (the learning phase presented in Table 2) we see the long memory characteristics we are expecting with this model. In the second phase (the commitment phase presented in Table 3) we fail to generate any long memory properties.

As soon as we switch off learning, these long memory phenomena disappear. It is not sufficient to have just the correct mix of strategies in order to generate long memory. So there is something about the dynamics of weight changing (caused in this case by the learning process) which is causing these phenomena.

Table 1. Default Values for All Models

Parameter	Value
Std dev of fundamental weight (σ_f)	1.5
Std dev of chartist weight (σ_c)	1.5
Std dev of noise weight (σ_n)	1.5
Probability of Mutating	0.08
Probability of entering the λ	1.0
Maximum markup or markdown (k_{max})	50%
Maximum period over which trends are calculated (l_{max})	100 units of time
Period over which price expectations are made (τ)	200 units of time
Fundamental price (F)	1000
Number of Traders	1000
Order Life	200 units of time
Tick Size (the smallest price differential)	0.1

Table 2. LY Model Learning Phase. Percentages of runs with long memory for volume, volatility, order signs and returns at various time lags ranging From 4×50 (200 units of time) to 10×50 (500 units of time).

Lag	Volume	Volatility	Order Signs	Returns
q=4	100	100	87	4
q=6	100	100	89	4
q=8	100	100	89	4
q=10	100	100	89	4

5 Model Stability

In this section we review the stability of the LY Model. We vary some of the free-parameters described earlier, the standard deviations of the Gaussian distributions from which the weights are chosen (Equation 9) and the mutation degree. The mutation degree is the probability that any individual will mutate it's strategy and draw a new weight from the distributions in (Equation 9). We have extended the experiment execution time to highlight any problems in stability with respect to time. The experiments were run for 10 times the default time (10 x 250000 units of time) and parameter values were

Table 3. LY Model Commitment. Percentages of runs with long memory for volume, volatility, order signs and returns at various time lags ranging From 4×50 (200 units of time) to 10×50 (500 units of time).

Lag	Volume	Volatility	Order Signs	Returns
q=4	0	0	0	0
q=6	0	0	0	0
q=8	0	0	0	0
q=10	0	0	0	0

Table 4. Ranges of Parameter Values

Parameter	Value
Std dev of fundamental weight (σ_f)	0.0 to 3.0
Std dev of chartist weight (σ_c)	0.0 to 3.0
Std dev of noise weight (σ_n)	0.0 to 3.0
Mutation Constant	0.05 to 0.20

randomly drawn (uniformly) from the ranges in Table 4. Fifty sets of random parameter variations were executed with 10 executions for each set (totalling 500 for 2500000 units of time). In Table 5 we present the results of the first experiment. We note we get negative results from the LY Model which produces weak Order Sign long memory but also long memory in returns (not a stylised fact of financial markets). In Tables 6 and 7 we have separated out the long memory properties of the execution of the LY Model into an early part of the test and a later part. We note that the long memory properties of the model are changing with respect to time. The state of the population in the LY Model converges to a relatively static steady-state. At the same time, the long memory properties of the market diminish; the long memory phenomena are not stable over time in the LY Model. In Table 8 we display the results for the execution of the LY Model with just the atomic extensions and finally in Table 9 we display the results for the Contrarian model. Comparing Tables 8 and 9 with the LY Model execution in Table 5 we see a substantial improvement in the stability of the Contrarian model over the LY model.

In Figure 2 the weight means of LY Model change relatively smoothly, the Contrarian Model (Figure 3), in contrast, is very much more dynamic, the mean values for fundamentalist and chartist are moving a great deal relative to the LY model. Comparing the bars (which indicate the fundamentalist SD (σ_f) and chartist SD (σ_c) with time) in Figure 2 and 3 we see that the LY Model fundamentalist and chartist weight distributions tend to converge while with the Contrarian Model the chartist weight distribution hardly converges at all and the fundamentalist distribution is diverging.

Table 5. Parameter Variation Experimental Results for LY Model. Percentages of runs with long memory for volume, volatility, order signs and returns at various time lags ranging From 4×50 (200 units of time) to 10×50 (500 units of time).

Lag	Volume	Volatility	Order Signs	Returns
q=4	76	86	18	12
q=6	76	83	18	14
q=8	76	82	18	14
q=10	75	81	18	15

Table 6. Early Phase Execution Results for LY Model. Percentages of runs with long memory for volume, volatility, order signs and returns at various time lags ranging From 4×50 (200 units of time) to 10×50 (500 units of time).

Lag	Volume	Volatility	Order Signs	Returns
q=4	100	99	50	50
q=6	100	99	52	55
q=8	100	99	53	57
q=10	100	99	54	61

Table 7. Later Phase Execution Results for LY Model. Percentages of runs with long memory for volume, volatility, order signs and returns at various time lags ranging From 4×50 (200 units of time) to 10×50 (500 units of time).

Lag	Volume	Volatility	Order Signs	Returns
q=4	69	79	27	25
q=6	70	77	28	28
q=8	70	76	29	29
q=10	70	75	29	31

We are seeing the convergence of the LY Model into a region in the strategy space. The GA in the LY model has been successful in finding a region in this space (the successful completion of its learning). The Contrarian Model is failing to converge in the strategy space. The LY Model is not generating stable long memory properties,

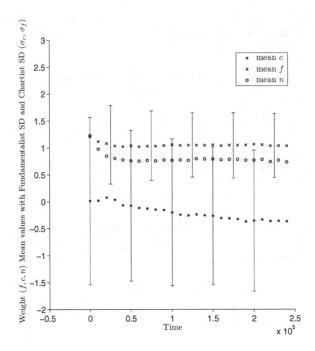

Fig. 2. LY Model. Mean Fundamentalist (f), Chartist (c) and Noise (n) weights with time and Fundamentalist and Chartist Standard Deviation (σ_f, σ_c)

Table 8. Experimental Results for Atomic Model. Percentages of runs with long memory for volume, volatility, order signs and returns at various time lags ranging From 4×50 (200 units of time) to 10×50 (500 units of time).

Lag	Volume	Volatility	Order Signs	Returns
q=4	96	90	43	0
q=6	96	89	41	0
q=8	96	89	40	0
q=10	96	89	39	1

because the successful genetic algorithm is converging to a region in the strategy space. By restructuring the agent strategy space and increasing contrarianism we are able to retain the dynamic necessary to produce stable long memory results (Tables 8 and 9).

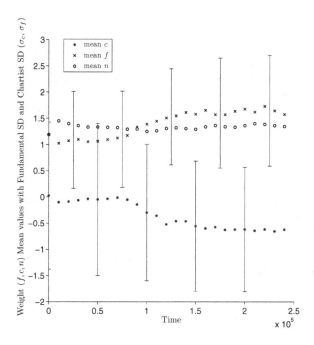

Fig. 3. Contrarian Model: Mean Fundamentalist (f), Chartist (c) and Noise (n) weights with time and Fundamentalist and Chartist Standard Deviation (σ_f, σ_c)

Table 9. Experimental Results for Contrarian Model. Percentages of runs with long memory for volume, volatility, order signs and returns at various time lags ranging From 4×50 (200 units of time) to 10×50 (500 units of time).

Lag	Volume	Volatility	Order Signs	Returns
q=4	94	93	58	0
q=6	94	92	58	0
q=8	93	91	58	0
q=10	92	91	58	0

6   Conclusion

While imitation may contribute to the generation of long memory phenomena in real financial markets other factors must play a role in producing stable long memory phenomena over time. Our model which incorporates contrarianism and strong disparity between strategies is able to generate a more dynamic behaviour in steady state, and is therefore able to produce more consistent long memory results across different free-parameter settings. The LY model [8,9] is not stable with respect to variation in free-parameter settings and model execution time. This was caused by the convergence of the Genetic Algorithm to a smaller and smaller strategy space and a loss, therefore, of the dynamic that causes the long memory phenomena. We modify the LY model adding atomic agents and increased contrarianism (the Contrarian Model) which retains the dynamic necessary to generate stable long memory phenomena (Section 5).

We conjecture that any model that causes and maintains a dynamic switching behaviour will produce stable long memory and that a non-learning heuristic model would also produce positive long memory phenomena; this is the subject of future research.

References

1. Cont, R.: Empirical Properties of Asset Returns: Stylised Facts and Statistical Issues. Quantitative Finance 1, 223–236 (2001)
2. Cont, R.: An Anatomy of Trading Strategies. The Review of Financial Studies 11(3), 489–519 (1998)
3. Ding, Z., Granger, C.W.J., Engle, R.F.: A Long Memory Property of Stock Market Returns and a New Model. Journal of Empirical Finance 1, 83–106 (1993)
4. Engle, R.F.: Autoregressive Conditional Heteroskedasticity with Estimates of the Variance of United Kingdom Inflation. Econometrica 50, 987–1008 (1982)
5. Evans, G.W., Honkapohja, S.: Learning and Expectations in Macroeconomics. Princeton University Press (2001)
6. Heemeijer, P., Hommes, C.H., Sonnemans, J., Tuinstra, J.: Forming Price Expectations in Positive and Negative Feedback Systems. Technical Report 04-15, Universiteit van Amsterdam (2004)
7. Lamoureux, C.G., Lastrapes, W.D.: Heteroskedasticity in Stock Return Data: Volume Versus GARCH Effects. Journal of Finance 45(1), 221–229 (1990)
8. LeBaron, B., Yamamoto, R.: Long-memory in an Order-Driven Market. Physica A 383, 85–89 (2007)
9. LeBaron, B., Yamamoto, R.: The Impact of Imitation on Long-Memory in an Order Driven Market. Eastern Economic Journal 34, 504–517 (2008)
10. Lillo, F., Mike, S., Farmer, J.D.: Theory for Long Memory in Supply and Demand. Physical Review E 7106, 287–297 (2005)
11. Lo, A.W.: Long-Term Memory in Stock Market Prices. Econometrica 59, 1279–1314 (1991)
12. Lobato, I., Velasco, C.: Long Memory in Stock-Market Trading Volume. Business and Economic Statistics 18(4), 410–426 (2000)
13. Mantegna, R.N., Stanley, E.H.: Stock Market Dynamics and Turbulence: Parallel Analysis of Fluctuation Phenomena. Physica A 239(1-3), 255–266 (1997)
14. Mantegna, R.N., Stanley, E.H.: Scaling Behavior in the Dynamics of an Economic Index. Nature 376, 46–49 (2002)
15. Pagan, A.: The Econometrics of Financial Markets. Journal of Empirical Finance 3(1), 15–102 (1996)

Autonomously Revising Knowledge-Based Recommendations through Item and User Information

Avi Rosenfeld, Aviad Levy, and Asher Yoskovitz

Jerusalem College of Technology, Jerusalem 91160, Israel
{rosenfa,aviadl}@jct.ac.il,
asher.yoskovitz@mysupermarket.com

Abstract. Recommender systems are now an integral part of many e-commerce websites, providing people relevant products they should consider purchasing. To date, many types of recommender systems have been proposed, with major categories belonging to item-based, user-based (collaborative) or knowledge-based algorithms. In this paper, we present a hybrid system that combines a knowledge based (KB) recommendation approach with a learning component that constantly assesses and updates the system's recommendations based on a collaborative and item based components. This combination facilitated creating a commercial system that was originally deployed as a KB system with only limited user data, but grew into a progressively more accurate system by using accumulated user data to augment the KB weights through item based and collaborative elements. This paper details the algorithms used to create the hybrid recommender, and details its initial pilot in recommending alternative products in an online shopping environment.

1 Introduction

Recommender systems have become an integral part of many e-commerce websites, giving consumers suggestions for additional or alternative products to purchase. These systems are part of well known websites such as Amazon.com, Pandora, Yahoo!, and Netflix [2–4, 7]. In fact, Netflix recently offered a Million Dollar Prize [2] for significantly increasing the quality of its recommendations, highlighting the importance of this field to e-commerce websites.

For commercial companies, recommendations are important to both directly and indirectly generate sales. Direct sales can be generated in two ways. First, a person may wish to buy a specific product from a website, but not be able to complete the transaction due to the product no longer being in stock. The recommender system can then provide alternate products, still completing a sale. In a second scenario, even if the product is in stock, the recommendation system may be able to provide additional items that the user may wish to buy, even furthering the revenue from the website. Even if the recommender system does not directly produce sales, they can be critical in providing an improved shopping experience thus attracting more shoppers to the website and indirectly producing more sales. In these types of scenarios, the recommender system can provide additional information about related products or services that might aid the user in better using a product they just purchased. In these types of cases, the recommender

E. David et al. (Eds.): AMEC/TADA 2011, LNBIP 119, pp. 57–70, 2013.

system can provide an after sales support system, ensuring the buyer is satisfied with the purchase.

In this paper, we describe the recommender system we built for the e-commerce website, mysupermarket.co.uk. MySupermarket is a relatively small private e-commerce company that makes its revenues by providing recommendations of grocery products to buy. All revenues are generated as a percentage of the total order places, so it is critical that the shopping experiences be as pleasant as possible, and recommendations be as relevant as possible, to boost sales. One of the key features of MySupermarket is its five ways it helps users save money[1]. The first and most important mechanism is a "swap and save" feature where the recommender system provides alternate (swap), yet similar, items to the user that are cheaper (save). This paper focuses on the algorithms involved with the recommender agent in this system.

The novelty of MySupermarket's swap and save agent lies in its combination of knowledge based, collaborative filtering and item based algorithms. In the next section, we details the background of the recommender algorithms upon which our hybrid system is based, and stress the contribution of this work. In Section 3, we describe My-Supermarket's current recommender agent, which integrates the expert's knowledge exclusively to produce recommendations. Unique to our system is a learning agent that creates recommendations based on the current expert recommendations, but also autonomously updates the expert's recommendation with item based and collaborative information. This approach is novel in that it presents the first hybrid of all major types of recommender technologies: knowledge, item based and collaborative. We detail this approach in Section 4. Section 5 concludes and provides directions for how this work can be generally applied to other systems as well.

2   Related Work

To date, two major groups of algorithms have been proposed for use in recommender systems, *collaborative* and *item based* approaches [1, 3, 5, 7, 10]. The term collaborative filtering was coined by the designers of one of the first of these systems, Tapestry [6], to capture that people often obtain information through collaborating with one another to obtain information. Systems based on collaborative approaches (also called user based) have been widely used in many commercial applications [2, 4–7] and facilitate giving a given user recommendations based on the past behavior of a known group of similar users. A second popular group of recommenders are item based (often called content based) approaches and focus on similarities between items to produce recommendations, typically based on the type of content of the item that is being search for [1, 4, 7, 10]. These approaches assume a generality between all types of users, and focus on shared characteristics between all members of the system. For example, assume preset categories exists for types of genre for books or movies (e.g. comedy, mystery, documentary, and classic). Once we have identified the genre of one item that is being searched for by all users, we can recommend other items of the same type. Theoretically there is no need within this approach to consider a given user's history once a categorization scheme has been implemented based on the item based approach.

---

[1] http://www.mysupermarket.co.uk/Help/FAQ.aspx/

One major disadvantage in both the collaborative and item based approaches is the time required and / or the needed data required to build these models. This is often referred to as the "cold start" or "ramp up" problems whereby the system cannot make effective recommendations at the beginning of its operation [4, 5, 7]. The "cold start" element within user based approaches refers to the challenge in a-priori knowing what this user, or similar users, will do in new or in the early stages of a given system. It can take weeks, or even months until enough data is collected on new items to attempt a collaborative solution. Even within item based approaches, it is not necessary clear which characteristics should be used to find similar items without any a-priori knowledge. This problem is very significant for MySupermarket as new products are constantly being added to the system and there is no clear connection between the new item and others in the database. Thus, alternative recommendation approaches are necessary.

A third, less popular approach, involves *knowledge based* recommendation [3, 5] which uses some preset rules for generating recommendations. The advantage of this approach is a complete solution to the cold-start problem – accurate recommendations can be immediately generated. The major disadvantage to this approach is the steep overhead involved with the knowledge engineering. MySupermarket currently employs 9 knowledge experts who create rules for generating recommendations for new products. Not only are these rules expensive to generate, but they are not necessarily accurate. The goal of this paper is to describe an approach that uses a knowledge based approach for the early stages of the system, but also create recommender agents that can autonomously update these initial recommendations based on both item based and collaborative approaches.

To the best of our knowledge, this paper represents the first of its kind – a knowledge based approach with item based and collaborative elements to update the original recommendations. Many hybrid recommendation models have been previously suggested with combinations of these approaches and surveys of these models have been previously published [1, 4, 5]. These algorithms often combine the two popular families of recommendation algorithms – collaborative and item-based approaches [1, 8]. Closest to our approach are the Libra [9] and MovieLens [11] systems. However, both of these systems augment collaborative systems with content based approaches. However, many other hybrid combinations are possible, with previous work described a theoretical number of 53 possible different types of hybrid systems [4]. The same article also points out that most theoretical combinations have not been studied or implemented, and particularly singles out directions involving hybrid systems with knowledge based components should be further explored. Particularly, our system goes one step further from previous hybrids, by also integrating expert knowledge along with a more classic content based – collaborative hybrid. We now detail the exact algorithms used by the system, and how the expert's recommendations are augmented by the item based and collaborative elements.

3   Using MySupermarket's Expert Data

As most recommendation systems are based on collaborative or item based data that can be cheaply obtained and analyzed [3, 5], it may seem strange that MySupermarket bases its system on a costly team of experts. In this section, we describe the motivation behind MySupermarket's business decision to use this approach, as well how the company uses this data in creating its recommendation system.

MySupermarket.com's use of experts to create recommendation system is indeed costly. The company employees a team of experts that evaluate thousands of products that are sold through the website, and create an expert measure which they call a *similarity score* which compares all products to each other. To slightly simplify the process, these experts defined "Product Families" of similar products such as types of wines, dairy product, diapers, etc., and only consider creating scores for all products within all given product families. Nonetheless, this process is expensive, as the company employees a team of 9 experts who on average study 100 products a day checking and updating products' similarity rating. The current trigger for this analysis is when new products are added for sale by MySupermarket, thus requiring the experts to reconsider how these new products are comparable to existing ones.

With the growth of automated recommendation systems, one might think that there is no longer a need for this costly knowledge engineering process and these experts should be replaced by automated recommendation agents. However, MySupermarket's use of these expert's knowledge goes well beyond its application for helping recommend products to end users, or its Business to Consumer (B2C) e-commerce website. In addition, these experts' knowledge forms the foundation for a second Business to Business (B2B) application, called MySupermarket insights that provides information about trends and possible strategic growth opportunities related to products supermarkets stock. While our focus is on how the recommendations from the first system can be improved, it should be noted that the second types of recommendations for businesses are no less important to the business strategy of the company and cannot be replaced by known recommendation algorithms. This is because the B2C application has already been functioning for several years and has now created enough historical data to overcome the classic cold start problem in new recommendation systems [4, 5]. However, the B2B application has far less historical data and the experts' knowledge is not easily encodable. For example, these experts maintain a blog about product trends and prices and thus cannot be replaced with automated agents. More about the B2B application, and the recommendations it provides can be found at the company's website at: http://www.mysupermarket-insights.co.uk/Marketing/Services.aspx.

In creating the B2C application, the expert's knowledge is central towards deciding what recommendations are presented to the user, and in generating what the company calls "swap recommendations". While shopping, items can be presented to the user that may be of interest, such as items that may save the user money by purchasing them in larger bulk, or alternative products that should be considered, especially when these items are discounted due to sales promotions or are a comparable generic alternative. Furthermore, these recommendations are especially important when the item they wished to buy is not in stock.

The expert's knowledge is then used in conjunction with item based data to create recommendations. Similar to item based recommendation systems, swap recommendations are generated by constructing a similarity vector between the desired product and characteristics of all other products within the company [1, 4, 7, 10]. However, non-hybrid item based recommenders are based on generic item data, which for this domain are likely to include characteristics like the product family, its quantity, price, weight, and color. In contrast, MySupermarket's hybrid system includes one new characteristic, the expert's similarity measure, and explicitly gives this item with very high weight in generating the vector to decide what products to recommend. Additionally, as opposed to classic item based methods that use machine learning techniques to decide how to weigh each characteristic within the vector, MySupermarket currently uses a hard-coded proprietary weight function between these items. For example, this weight system presents up to 5 recommendation if it finds items that are comparable based on these hard-coded weights taking into account all item's characteristics. In addition, MySupermarket also leaves one field, the last recommendation, where recommendations are based only one characteristic, price alone. Here, the system always presents an alternative if a cheaper generic substitute exists in the product database even if it is not deemed as similar by the other characteristics.

To better understand the system, please see Figure 1 depicting a screen shot from the company's website. Note that in the screenshot the user is given up to four swap recommendations by the system. Only items that are deemed worthy based on this weight function are presented to the user, and thus the full maximal number of 6 recommendations were not presented here. Please note in the first row of Figure 1 that the user is encouraged to consider buying similar diapers in bulk, with the first choice being cheaper than the second, but both being the same brand as the original product, and only then is the user presented a third choice that is a different generic brand, yet far cheaper. In the second row, the user is informed that there is a buy one get one free sale on the item they selected, and she can receive a second product for no additional price. Here no additional products are presented, as the expert's hard coded threshold decides no other products are sufficiently similar given the price differences. Similarly, in the third row, the user is informed there is a sale and she could save money per item if she chooses to buy 2 products instead of one, but no other products are given from different brand. In the last row, the user is again encouraged to consider a sale item or a generic substitute for the selected item.

4   Creating a New Type of Hybrid System

One important question MySupermarket must address is how good are the system's recommendations, and if they are not always effective, how could they be improved? Intuitively, it seems unlikely that the system of static weights described above will always be accurate, especially as the items in the product database are constantly in flux, as sales and changes in stock are frequent. Thus, these static weights do not necessarily have the ability to deal with these dynamics. Furthermore, the need to constantly update these weights is costly. Clearly some mechanism is needed to autonomously update the system.

Towards building a more effective system, we believe a new type of hybrid model is needed, as presented in this section. The basis of this hybrid is the above knowledge based system, which is useful for providing initial recommendations and is critical for other MySupermarket applications. However, once a sufficient history is stored through system use, item based and collaborative components can be potentially useful in improving the system. However, one key question that must be addressed is when and how can this data be useful in improving the system. Thus, care must be taken to properly evaluate the usefulness of this added information, as we now detail.

Fig. 1. A Sample Webpage from MySupermarket's Website

4.1   A High Level System Overview

We propose constructing a three pronged hybrid that is knowledge based, but uses item based and collaborative elements. A high level overview of our solution is shown in Figure 3. As per MySupermarket's business model, the Knowledge Based component is at the core of the system and is shown at the top left corner of the diagram. As people begin using the system, historical data is accumulated and this data is sent as input into item based and collaborative components. If this data is found to be useful, a hybrid model is formed where these models can be used in several ways: First, and on the most basic level, assuming the expert's knowledge is not equivalent to these models, we can manually query the expert for input. It may be the expert will then wish to manually revise or accept the values automatically generated by these components. However, as we have begun to find, the experts are willing to forgo this step, thus automatically accepting the autonomously generated agent changes. The outcome is a revised hybrid system, that began exclusively as being knowledge based, but has accepted many key components from the item based and collaborative algorithms.

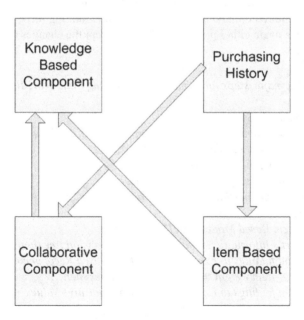

Fig. 2. An architecture of a Hybrid Recommender System that is based on expert knowledge, but also revises the system with item-based and collaborative components

To better understand the process by which the knowledge based recommender is modified, please refer to Algorithm 1. As lines 1 and 2 state, initially the experts must manually evaluate every item within the system, assigning a similarity value for every product versus all other products. This similarity values is then evaluated in conjunction with all other item attributes in a hard-coded formula to produce the system's initial recommendations. However, as the system is used, some critical size of product history is likely to become available for this product (line 5), to reevaluate these initial knowledge based recommendations. Assuming this is the case, we currently perform three checks. First, in line 6, we evaluate the overall effectiveness for the recommendation output of this product. We found that for many products the users were willing to accept the system's recommendations, and for others users almost never accepted the system's recommendation. Currently, we simply flag those products with a very low user acceptance of the system's recommendations (line 6) and present these results to the experts for consideration. However, our goal is to automate any such evaluations through allowing the recommender agents to autonomously change the system. To accomplish this, we use verify and change the system through item-based and collaborative data when available. In line 8, agents automatically evaluate the effectiveness of the expert's hard-coded initial weights through machine learning techniques, e.g. decision trees, as described in the next subsection. Assuming this item-based model is not built around the expert's information (line 9), the system can either prompt the expert to accept the item based recommendations or as we have begun to allow, autonomously update the system (line 10). Furthermore, the recommender agent checks the initial expert's recommendations against acquired collaborative data (line 11). Assuming these weights are not equal (line 12), we again either prompt the user to accept the changes or automatically update the system.

Algorithm 1. *The major steps for dynamically updating / changing the recommendation system*
01 **for** *Every product in System* **do**
02   *Create initial recommendations based on Expert's Knowledge*
03 **while** *the System is in use* **do**
04   **for** *Every product in System* **do**
05   **if** *data history exists for this product* **then**
06   **if** *User acceptance for product* < *threshold* **then**
07   *Flag product in system*
08   *Build Item Based Model with Decision trees*
09   **if** *Expert's Information not the root of the decision tree* **then**
10   *Present findings to Expert / Accept Item Based Recommendations*
11   **if** *Hybrid-Item weight* ≠ *Collaborative Values* **then**
12   *Present findings to Expert / Accept Collaborative Values*

As Algorithm 1 indicates, the recommender system is one in flux, beginning exclusively based on expert knowledge, but allows agents to autonomously update the initial system. However, in doing so, several challenges exist with implementing this algorithm, which are addressed in the following subsection. All three system checks of the expert's initial recommendations (lines 6 – 12) are built around the assumption that the recommender system can be objectively be evaluated. However, as we present in the next Section (4.2), evaluating recommender systems is far from trivial, especially if a controlled dataset cannot be formed. Second, we present a novel approach where agents can check the expert's recommendations using item based information. This again is not simple, and our approach for doing so is presented in Section 4.3. Finally, the use of collaborative data is again non-trivial, and our approach for doing so is presented in Section 4.4.

4.2 Evaluating the Overall System

MySupermarket's B2B and B2C applications are both built on their experts' knowledge. Thus, the key question about the accuracy of the expert's knowledge is not limited to the recommendations for their e-commerce website, but also for their B2B application as well. In general, many metrics have been proposed to date to evaluate the effectiveness of recommendation systems [7]. For example, one popular choice, used in the Netflix competition [2] is to use the root mean error level of prediction between a set of previously tagged known ratings that people provide, and a set of automatically generated recommendations by the system. However, this possibility is not available to us, as we have no previously tagged data to use as a baseline. Instead, we use the bottom line user satisfaction measure most intuitive to use in commercial systems [7].

We propose that two types of bottom line measures are useful in evaluating the expert's knowledge of this system. The first, and possibly more intuitive measure is to measure the number of purchases made because of the recommended product swaps. As the company has logged all transactions to its website over the past 5 years, extensive historical data is available to allow for this analysis. A second complementary measure searches for statistical correlation between those elements that were swapped in the past (line 5 of Algorithm 5) and the expert's recommendations. Note that the two studies are intrinsically linked: If no swaps are performed, the recommendation system is clearly not producing quality alternatives, and no correlation will be found between people's decisions and their swap purchases. If swaps are frequently performed, the question then becomes, "why"? Are these swaps due to something inherent with these products, or due to the expert's knowledge, both factors, or something else?

We found that the number of swap purchases made varied greatly between different product families. Figure 2 presents a look at 5 different product families and their average number of executed "swaps" or acceptance of the system's recommendation. Note that these 5 product families are a small samples of the 950 product families within the system. However, we did find overall great differences in the acceptance of the system's recommendations across different types of products. Intuitively, such differences may be because people are naturally more picky about accepting certain product substitutions other others. For example, we found that people looking to buy a certain type of dental accessories (e.g. dental floss) were most likely to accept the system's recommendation and chose an alternate product approximately 80% of the time. However, people who were looking to buy a certain type of insecticide were only nearly 60% likely to accept the system's recommendation, and people looking for hand cream were accepted the system's recommendation about 40% of the time. The percentage of times users accepted certain recommendations were extremely low, such as slightly more than 20% for chocolate mints, and less than even 5% for soup mixes. Overall we found that these examples represent a wide range of acceptance levels, and that people accepted the system's recommendations approximately 35% of the time. However, is this level

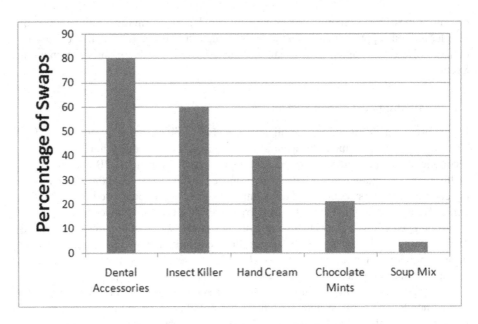

Fig. 3. Five Different Product Families and their Average Number of Accepted Recommendations

of success due to some inherent pickiness of users about some types of products versus others, or is this the truly optimal state? If it is not the optimal state, what changes would be necessary to further improve the system's performance?

At present, MySupermarket uses this swap analysis to create a report to the experts. The experts are then asked to manually analyze the data to question if their knowledge is in fact effective in generating more sale. For example, we may present the system's 5% success in generating swaps for soup mixes and ask the expert to manually change its recommendation scheme for the products in this group. However, the company's vision involves using autonomous agents to automatically update these expert's values, as described in the following sections.

4.3   Evaluating the System with Item Data

Our first goal was to verify and update the expert's similarity measure through using machine learning techniques to check the predictive ability of the expert's information. To do so, we use the well recognized Weka [12] package to create a predictive model regarding when people purchased a product from the among the system's recommendations. Realistically, some complex relationship likely exists between the type of product, the quality of the expert's information, the possible savings to the user, and other factors in determining if a swap purchase is made. For example, this analysis may find that price is used for some categories, other products are only swapped when the expert's similarity measure is less than a certain amount, and certain products are never swapped.

The use of machine learning techniques to validate the recommendation model is a twist from the classic use of these algorithms within item based recommenders. In classic item-based classification, a collection of all item characteristics are used in conjunction with historical data about purchases to create a learned model that correlates between the two [10]. This type of learning can use any machine learning algorithm, including Bayes, decision trees, and nearest neighbor methods to accurate find a correlation between items, their characteristics, and historical data. No a-priori assumption is made as to which characteristics will make the best model – in fact the purpose of the model is to find these characteristics. In contrast, our goal is exactly the opposite. The expert has already decided and hard-coded her own similarity measure as being most important, and fixed the relative value of all other item characteristics. In the best case scenario, the expert has discovered certain domain specific knowledge, encapsulated in its similarity measure, allowing it to surpass the recommendations of a pure item based system. Alternatively, the item based rules may approximate the expert based knowledge, and comparing the derived rules will allow us to confirm the accuracy of the expert knowledge. However, the pure item based system might be more accurate, allowing us to pinpoint for exactly which items the expert's knowledge is less accurate.

We chose to evaluate the expert's knowledge through creating a model based on decision trees. The advantage towards using trees versus any other model is that Weka [12] not only creates a machine learning model, but also outputs the exact rules used in this model. Assuming the expert's knowledge is critical to the system, one would expect to find the expert's similarity measure to be the key rule, or at the root of the decision tree. If the expert's knowledge is not effective, one would expect it to either not appear in the tree, or be limited to only very specific instances.

In creating these decision trees, we used as input the history of people's swap purchases for given product families, and entered all items' data into Weka [12]. The item's input data included information the expert's similarity measure, the projected saving by choosing the new item, as well as items characteristics not currently given significant weight by the expects, such as the serial number of the product and the serial number of the proposed product. We recognize that it is quite possible that items the overlooked, say the serial number of the proposed product, may produce recommendations that the experts overlooked.

For many product families, we were able to confirm the importance of the expert's knowledge, while for other products the expert's knowledge seemed much less important. For example, Weka's decision tree for purchases made for squash had at the root of the tree: similarity $<= 1.25$, or if the similarity measure is less than 1.25, then people are likely to buy in certain conditions. In other product families, such as for milk products, the similarity function was of secondary importance to the difference in cost between products. Here we found the rule: If the AlternativePrice < 0.85 and similarity < 1.1, then given certain other conditions the person will purchase the product. However, for other product families similarity had seemingly no significance. For example, for toilet paper the root rule was if the OriginalPricePerUnit $<= 0.35$ and the AlternativePricePerUnit $<= 0.28$, then a person will buy given other conditions. Thus, we found that using decision trees were useful in automatically generating where the expert's knowledge was most useful.

Note that as per line 9 of Algorithm 1, two possibilities exist when decision trees found that the expert's similarity measure was not the most important item characteristic. Until recently, this information was presented to the expert, who could then decide if she would like to revise the values, or accept the decision tree's rules instead. However, we have begun a pilot whereby the agent autonomously updates the expert's recommendation, especially for products where the expert's recommendations yielded a low recommendation (e.g. set the threshold of line 6 of Algorithm 1 to 10%).

4.4 Evaluating the System with Collaborative Data

We also use historical data to create a collaborative model to augment the expert's recommendations. The above machine learning approach to validate the expert's similarity measure can validate the importance of this item to the recommender agent for how the average, or typical user, behaved. Furthermore, the weights set by the expert, and even by the hybrid knowledge-item based system, are still uniform across all users. However, this approach does not validate how a specific user behaved, and if this model is appropriate for a specific user. For example, the experts may have hard-coded the system to only present alternatives where a similarity value of 1.0 or less is found. However, it may be found that certain users are willing to buy items that are even less similar (e.g. values of greater than 1.0) and some are more discriminating and only purchase items that are far more similar (say similarity 0.5 or less). Thus, the above approach can only verify that user's in general are willing to make purchases based on the expert's measures, it cannot predict if a specific user deviates from this assumption.

Note that the difference of the behavior of a general user and the behavior of a specific user is the inherent difference between item-based and collaborative recommendation systems. As our goal is to customize the system's recommendations as much as possible, we present a heuristic approach where the hybrid knowledge-item based agent's recommendations are further customized based on that specific user's history.

In general, we found that users generally decide to purchase a product based on the expert's similarity measure and the potential cost savings of the new item. However, while we found that these two attributes were important across all users, and thus formed an effective hybrid item-knowledge based system, the actually savings and similarity measures used by a specific user could differ greatly. To address this issue, we found that an heuristic approach, where the similarity and savings measures were tuned based on a specific user's past activity for a given product, was highly effective in improving the system's recommendations. This led to an effective automatic tuning of these parameters, increasing the companies sales through customers' swaps.

In general, it is important to stress that the company's experts were initially extremely hesitate to forgo their initial values in favor of these found by the item based and collaborative elements as described in the paper. This issue is further complicated by the fact that the system lacks any proper evaluating dataset, and thus it was extremely difficult to convince the experts of the importance of the agent's recommendations. We overcame this obstacle by first revising the systems only for those products where the initial success of the expert's system was extremely low (see line 6 of Algorithm 1). This work is ongoing, and will take nearly a year before we can quantify where this approach was successful. However, the generality of this approach leads and our initial feedback from the company's experts have led us to be confident about its importance.

5   Conclusions and Future Work

In this paper we introduced a novel hybrid approach to combine a knowledge based recommender system with item based and collaborative filtering elements. The system's recommender agent begins with a system exclusively based on the expert's knowledge, thus avoiding the classic cold start problem. However, as the system is used, a progressively larger history of user transactions are recorded. The system then uses this information to create hybrid models with item and collaborative items. An item based model is used to validate or even replace the user's knowledge. We describe using a novel variation of machine learning techniques to create a classic item based model can be used to validate the expert's knowledge. When the item based model finds the expert's knowledge is at the root of the item based model, the expert's knowledge is accepted. When it is found to not be a critical item in the model, the system can prompt the expert to update item data, or automatically replace and update the user's knowledge. Additionally, if the expert's knowledge is validated by the item based model, collaborative models are useful for further improving the system's recommendations by automatically tweaking the system's item's parameters based on a specific user's purchases. We present the system's prototype implementation and initial results demonstrating the importance and success of this approach.

Several related problems are worthy of future consideration. One key hurdle we needed to overcome was convincing the data experts that the agent's item and collaborative recommendations should replace or augment their own. We hope to further study at what point can one assume the agent's recommendations are definitive, and how to convince the experts of this. Achieving this goals would significantly aid us in the goal of fully automating system revisions. Additionally, we hope to further address how the system's evaluation can be better automated without explicitly labeled data as is done in many classic recommendation system's, such as the Netflix challenge [2]. We believe the approach we present, of using machine learning techniques to create an item based approach for evaluation, can be further generalized to address this point. The importance of hybrid systems such as the knowledge, item and collaborative system we present, are likely to be of significance to other areas and fields as well. It is likely that use of expert information can help avoid the "cold start" problem in other problems as well. Our model, where collaborative and item based information are later used, are likely to be equally useful for these problems as well. We hope to study what modifications to our approach are necessary, if any, in addressing new problems.

References

1. Adomavicius, G., Tuzhilin, A.: Toward the next generation of recommender systems: A survey of the state-of-the-art and possible extensions. IEEE Transactions on Knowledge and Data Engineering 17(6), 734–749 (2005)

2. Bennett, J., Lanning, S.: The netflix prize. In: KDD Cup and Workshop in Conjunction with KDD, pp. 3–6 (2007)
3. Burke, R.: Knowledge-based Recommender Systems. In: Encyclopedia of Library and Information Systems, vol. 69 (2000)
4. Burke, R.D.: Hybrid recommender systems: Survey and experiments. User Model and User-Adapted Interaction 12(4), 331–370 (2002)
5. Burke, R.: Hybrid Web Recommender Systems. In: Brusilovsky, P., Kobsa, A., Nejdl, W. (eds.) The Adaptive Web. LNCS, vol. 4321, pp. 377–408. Springer, Heidelberg (2007)
6. Goldberg, D., Nichols, D., Oki, B.M., Terry, D.: Using collaborative filtering to weave an information tapestry. Commun. ACM 35, 61–70 (1992)
7. Herlocker, J.L., Konstan, J.A., Terveen, L.G., Riedl, J.T.: Evaluating collaborative filtering recommender systems. ACM Trans. Inf. Syst. 22, 5–53 (2004)
8. Melville, P., Mooney, R.J., Nagarajan, R.: Content-boosted collaborative filtering for improved recommendations. In: Eighteenth National Conference on Artificial Intelligence, pp. 187–192. American Association for Artificial Intelligence (2002)
9. Melville, P., Mooney, R.J., Nagarajan, R.: Content-boosted collaborative filtering for improved recommendations. In: Eighteenth National Conference on Artificial Intelligence, pp. 187–192. American Association for Artificial Intelligence, Menlo Park (2002)
10. Pazzani, M., Billsus, D.: Content-Based Recommendation Systems, pp. 325–341 (2007)
11. Sarwar, B.M., Konstan, J.A., Borchers, A., Herlocker, J., Miller, B., Riedl, J.: Using filtering agents to improve prediction quality in the grouplens research collaborative filtering system. In: Proceedings of the 1998 ACM Conference on Computer Supported Cooperative Work, CSCW 1998, pp. 345–354 (1998)
12. Witten, I.H., Frank, E.: Data Mining: Practical Machine Learning Tools and Techniques, 2nd edn. Morgan Kaufmann (2005)

A Bidding Agent for Advertisement Auctions: An Overview of the CrocodileAgent 2010

Irena Siranovic, Tomislav Cavka, Ana Petric, and Vedran Podobnik

University of Zagreb, Faculty of Electrical Engineering and Computing
Zagreb, Croatia
{irenasiranovic,tomislavcavka1}@gmail.com,
{ana.petric,vedran.podobnik}@fer.hr

Abstract. Sponsored search is a popular form of targeted online advertising and the most profitable online advertising revenue format. Online publishers use different formats of unit price auctions to sell advertising slots. In the Trading Agent Competition Ad Auctions (TAC/AA) game, intelligent software agents represent a publisher which conduct keyword auctions and advertisers which participate in those auctions. The publisher is designed by game creators while advertisers are designed by game entrants. Advertisers bid for the placement of their ads on the publisher's web page and the main challenge placed before them is how to determine the right amount they should bid for a certain keyword. In this paper, we present the CrocodileAgent, our entry in the 2010 TAC AA Tournament. The agent's architecture is presented and a series of controlled experiments are discussed.

Keywords: trading agents, sponsored search, keyword auctions.

1 Introduction

Internet advertising provides a significant income stream for online publishers. Revenue of major search engines such as Google[1], Yahoo![2] and MSN[3] amounts to tens of billions of dollars annually (e.g., in 2010, Google reported total advertising revenues over USD $28 billion[4]). According to the report[5] published by the Interactive Advertising Bureau[6] and PricewaterhouseCoopers LLP[7], sponsored search is the most profitable online advertising revenue format which accounted for 47% of the total Internet advertisement revenue in the USA in the first half of 2010. In sponsored search (i.e., keyword advertising) publishers (i.e., search engines) use different formats [1] of unit price auctions (e.g., keyword auctions) to sell advertising slots (i.e., positions in the list that contains search results) [2].

---

[1] http://www.google.com/
[2] http://www.yahoo.com/
[3] http://www.msn.com/
[4] http://investor.google.com/financial/tables.html
[5] http://www.iab.net/media/file/IAB_report_1H_2010_Final.pdf
[6] http://www.iab.net/
[7] http://www.pwc.com/

E. David et al. (Eds.): AMEC/TADA 2011, LNBIP 119, pp. 71–86, 2013.
© Springer-Verlag Berlin Heidelberg 2013

In a keyword auction advertisers bid for the placement of their ads (i.e., rank of the ad in the results of the sponsored search) which are then displayed on the publisher's web page. The format of sponsored search results is very much alike the format of generic search results. Usually, it is comprised of the title of the ad, a short description and a hyperlink to the advertiser's web page or the web page of the advertised product. An ad is chosen for a specific keyword(s) from the user's query, thus targeting users interested in advertiser's products.

A publisher conducts keyword auctions and solicits bids. When a user submits a query containing one or more keywords, sponsored ads are displayed to the user alongside the results of a generic search mechanism. At the end of an auction, the publisher ranks advertisers' bids (i.e., determines the placement of their ads and the cost-per-click (CPC) for those ads) [3]. CPC is the price that an advertiser pays to the publisher each time its ad is clicked on.

According to earlier studies on user behaviour (e.g., [4]) the higher the position of the search result (e.g., ad, document) is, the users will be more likely to click on it. This phenomenon, where the probability that the result will be clicked depends not only on its relevance, but also on its position in the search results, is known as the position bias. Several models of the position bias have been proposed and the cascade model gave the best explanation for the position bias in early ranks [5]. However, the latest research has shown that 46% of the users do not click sequentially (i.e., start from the best ranked result and continue to lower ranked ones) and 57% of them do not behave as suggested by the cascade model (i.e., first click on the higher and afterwards on the lower positioned results) [6].

A challenge placed upon publishers evolves around the selection of a mechanism which will result with highest profits. There are two frequently used mechanisms for ranking solicited bids: i) rank-by-bid, and, ii) rank-by-revenue. As the name of the rank-by-bid mechanism states the bids are sorted in a descending order (i.e., the bids offering a higher CPC get higher ranked positions), while the rank-by-revenue mechanism multiplies the offered CPC with the ad's expected relevance (i.e., the percentage of users that will click on the ad once it is displayed to them) and afterwards sorts bids in a descending order of the calculated product [7]. In addition, some mechanisms offer advertisers the possibility to target a certain group of users by specifying the context for viewing ads (e.g., user's location, time of day) and to control exposure by limiting the number of times an ad should be displayed to users [8].

From the advertisers' point of view, the question is how to determine the right amount they should bid for a certain keyword(s) since the probability that their ad will be better ranked than other ads rises as they place higher bids [9]. The complexity of the answer to this question increases as the availability of information about user behaviour, as well as bidding behaviour of other advertisers decreases.

The paper is organized as follows. Section 2 describes the characteristics of the Trading Agent Competition Ad Auctions (TAC/AA) game. A brief overview of the research in the area of TAC/AA bidding strategies is given in Section 3. Section 4 presents the CrocodileAgent 2010, our entrant in the 2010 TAC/AA Tournament. Section 5 presents the conducted experiments and the obtained results, while Section 6 concludes the paper and gives an outline for future work.

2 TAC/AA Game

Researchers test advertisers' bidding strategies by using the designed market simulators which provide a risk free environment [10]. The TAC/AA game [11,12], which was released in 2009, is based on such a market simulator. In other TAC games market simulators are used to find perspective solutions for the supply chain management problem [13,14,15], market design problem [6,16,17] and energy trading in smart grid environments [18].

The TAC/AA game enables advertisers to bid on multiple queries and to define budget constraints in an information-lacking and competitive environment. Eight intelligent program agents which represent online advertisers participate in the game. Each advertiser sells 9 different products which are specified by the manufacturer (i.e., Flat, Lioneer and PG) and the component (i.e., TV, Audio and DVD). Furthermore, each advertiser is specialized for one manufacturer and for one component type.

The ad ranking mechanism varies between rank-by-bid and rank-by-revenue [19] and is chosen at the beginning of each game. Users can generate 9 different queries by specifying both manufacturer and component (i.e., F2 level query), 6 different queries by specifying only manufacturer or component (i.e., F1 level query) and one query where neither manufacturer nor component are specified (i.e., F0 level query). Correspondingly, the conversion probability increases as more keywords are specified in the query. Users can find themselves in one of the following states: i) non-searching, ii) searching, and, iii) transacted; while the user population in each state (and sub-state) is modelled as a Markov chain.

In the TAC/AA game scenario, when a user submits a query, an auction for the given keyword(s) starts. The auction is an instance of the repeated generalized second price auction (i.e., the price that the advertiser pays for the position of its ad is determined by the price which was offered by the winner of the next-best position in its bid) and the first position is allocated to the bidder with the highest bid. An advertiser sends a bid bundle (i.e., one bid for each query class) to the publisher every day. A bid consists of: i) the CPC an advertiser is ready to pay, ii) the chosen ad which can be generic or targeted (i.e., specified manufacturer and/or component), iii) budget limits for each query class, and, iv) budget limit for all queries altogether for the following day (optional). The publisher uses the information from the bids when it runs ad auctions for the received user queries. Advertisers receive daily reports about the outcomes of the prior (i.e., two days old) auctions and use those information to generate new bids. Daily reports include: i) query report, ii) account status report, and, iii) sales report. The game lasts 60 virtual days.

3 Related Work

The bidding strategy for keyword auctions has been a great challenge for researchers that conducted various simulations and empirical analyses on this matter. Berg *et.al.* [20] have presented autonomous bidding strategies for ad auctions which are based on click probability and the CPC estimations. They use two kind of algorithms for bid optimization: i) rule-based algorithms, and, ii) greedy multiple choice Knapsack algorithms. Pardoe and Stone [21] have shown a particle filter that can be used for estimating other agents' bids given a periodic ranking of their bids. The particle filter is used for estimating bids of other advertisers. Since the information revealed about competing advertisers is limited, they have shown how such models can learn from the past bidding data. Cigler [22] has described several bidding strategies (Return-on-investment (ROI), Knapsack ROI, Balanced Best-response, online Knapsack) and evaluated their performance empirically. The best performing strategies were ROI and Balanced Best-response. Furthermore, Cigler presented a new profit maximizing strategy for multiple keyword ad campaigns that takes into account the budged constraint and has shown to be successful particularly for small budgets.

4   CrocodileAgent 2010

With an intention to better investigate strategic approaches to ad auctions mechanisms, an advertiser agent CrocodileAgent has been designed. A bidding strategy was chosen among several strategies (i.e., profit maximization, linear regression) [23] and analysed through controlled experiments. The CrocodileAgent's bidding model used for participating in ad auctions is shown in Figure 1 and can be divided into three logical segments: i) the ad generator, ii) the CPC generator, and, iii) the daily spend limit generator.

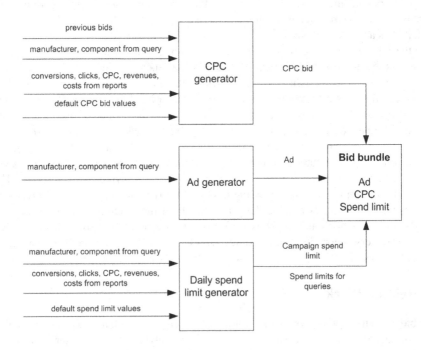

Fig. 1. CrocodileAgent's bidding model

4.1   The ad Generator Algorithm

The method chosen for ad generation is based on query focus levels and is shown in Algorithm 1. This method was chosen by analysing final results in game simulations with several different implemented algorithms for ad generation. The results shown that the conversion probability is the highest when a user submits a query with the focus level F2. Since there are 9 different products and each user has a preference for just one of them, it is highly probable that a user will click on the ad that matches the query when he/she submits an F2 query. Furthermore, we have concluded that if an agent provides the generic ad for the submitted F2 query, the probability that the user will click on the ad decreases significantly, especially if competing agents chose one of targeted ads.

Algorithm 1. CrocodileAgent's ad generation algorithm

---

if *query focus level = F0 or F1* **then**
    generated ad = generic
else
    generated ad = targeted (F2 manufacturer, F2 component)
end

For a submitted F1 query, the CrocodileAgent generates generic ads – if the CrocodileAgent generated a targeted ad, it would have to decide which component or manufacturer to add alongside the specified keyword (i.e., manufacturer or component, respectively). The negative aspect of the latter approach is that the targeted ad has to match user preferences in order to accomplish a conversion (the probability that the generated ad matches user preferences is 1/3). If the ad does not match user preferences, the click probability decreases according to the targeting factor [11], and vice versa. Moreover, if the ad does not match user preferences, the user may click on the ad, but he/she will not convert and thus he/she will only increases the agent's cost. On the other hand, the benefit of the approach that results with a targeted ad manifests in case when the ad matches the submitted query – positive aspects of this approach are: i) additional profit gained by component through component specialization bonus (CSB) or manufacturer specialization bonus (MSB), ii) increased odds of converting based on CSB, and, iii) increased targeting effect.

4.2   The CPC Generator Algorithm

The CPC bid is defined for every query type with an intention to maximize the profit (profit = revenue - cost). Taking into consideration the two days old information in the received reports, the algorithm for generating the CPC for the first two days of the game contains fixed values of CPC. Values for all query types are defined based on matches between the component and manufacturer in a query and agent's specialties as shown in Algorithm 2.

Algorithm 2. CrocodileAgent's initial bidding algorithm

$result$ = match between query and agents specialties;
switch $result$ **do**
    case *miss*
        $bid = \alpha$;
    case *miss-neutral*
        $bid = \beta$;
    case *miss-hit*
        $bid = \gamma$;
    case *neutral*
        $bid = \delta$;
    case *neutral-hit*
        $bid = \epsilon$;
    case *hit*
        $bid = \xi$;
endsw
where $\beta < \gamma < \alpha \leq \delta \leq \epsilon < \xi$;

The more accurate the match is, the higher the bid is. Additionally, the values are scaled by agent's capacity (i.e., the bid is slightly decreased in case of medium or low capacity). Definitions of matching values are listed in Table 1, while Table 2 contains the parameter values. All parameter values were determined by using a heuristic approach. The decisions were based on conducted game simulations (locally and in the TAC/AA 2010 qualifying rounds) by comparing the CrocodileAgent's profit for different sets of parameters used.

Table 1. Definitions of specialty matching values

Value	Query type	Definition
miss	F2	Component and manufacturer from query do not match agent's specialties.
miss-neutral	F1	Component or manufacturer from query does not match agent's specialties, second keyword is null.
miss-hit	F2	Component or manufacturer from query does not match agent's specialties, second keyword is a match.
neutral	F0	A query without specified manufacturer and component.
neutral-hit	F1	Component or manufacturer from query matches agent's specialties, second keyword is null.
hit	F2	Component and manufacturer from query are agent's specialties.

A method for defining the CPC bids in the remainder of the game is based on the calculations of the conversion rate (i.e., the ratio of average number of clicks to conversions). If the rate is satisfactory, the new bid is based on the CPC bid from two days ago. Otherwise, the new bid is based on the CPC that the agent actually paid. The bid is

Table 2. Values of parameters for initial bidding

Parameter	α	β	γ	δ	ϵ	ξ
Value	1.15	0.65	1.05	1.15	1.15	1.25

later adjusted depending on the query focus level and the CrocodileAgent's specialties.
The CPC generator algorithm is shown in Algorithm 3.

Algorithm 3. CrocodileAgent's CPC generator algorithm

$revenue$ = last revenue for a query received in report;
n_{click} = average number of clicks per day;
$n_{conversion}$ = average number of conversions per day;
$query_{fl}$ = query focus level;
$result$ = match between query and agent's specialties;

if $revenue \neq 0$ **then**
    $mod = n_{click}/n_{conversion}$;
    $bid = \texttt{DefineBid}(mod)$;

    if $query_{fl} == F0$ *or* $query_{fl} == F1$ **then**
        $bid = focus\ level\ parameter \cdot bid$
    end

    if $result == hit$ **then**
        $bid = specialty\ parameter \cdot last\ paid\ bid$
    end
else
    if $query_{fl} == F2$ **then**
        $bid = \min(minimum\ bid\ zero, hit\ parameter \cdot last\ bid_{day-2})$;
        if $manufacturer\ and\ component\ of\ query == agent's\ specialties$ **then**
            $bid = specialty\ parameter\ zero \cdot bid$
        end
    else
        $bid = parameter\ zero \cdot last\ bid_{day-2}$;
    end
end

function $\texttt{DefineBid}(mod)$

if $mod < ratio\ lower\ bound$ **then**
    $bid = \max(minimum\ bid, decrease\ factor \cdot last\ bid_{day-2})$;
else if $ratio\ lower\ bound \leq mod \leq ratio\ middle\ value$ **then**
    $bid = \max(minimum\ bid, increase\ factor \cdot last\ paid\ bid)$;
else
    $bid = \max(minimum\ bid, max\ increase\ factor \cdot last\ paid\ bid)$;
end
return bid;

Table 3. Values of bidding parameters during a game

Parameter	Definition	Value
ratio lower bound		10
ratio middle value		0.65
minimum bid	minimum CPC that an agent will bid	0.10
decrease factor	decrease factor in case of very good mod	0.97
increase factor	increase factor in case of average mod	1.15
max increase factor	increase factor in case of very bad mod	1.20
focus level parameter		0.80
speciality parameter		1.30
minimum bid zero	minimum CPC that an agent will bid in case that last revenue was zero	0.30
hit parameter		1.30
speciality parameter zero		1.20
parameter zero	a parameter used when agent's last revenue was zero	1.05

When determining CPC bids the most important aspect is the "quality" of an ad, which is measurable through the agent's profit. The quality of an ad is defined as an estimation that the user's click on that ad will turn into a conversion. The CrocodileAgent's bidding strategy does not change during the game. Table 3 contains the parameters that gave the most satisfactory results in the conducted experiments.

4.3   The Spend Limit Manager

General Spend Limit. Too many conversions lead to decrease of the possible conversions in the future due to stock shortage, as defined by the game rules [12]. The stock management policy is necessary since it can happen that a certain amount of products must be immediately available in order to avoid significant profit loss. On the other hand, excessive product storage becomes "dead capital". Additionally, the other driver for using spend limits are the clicks generated by informational searchers.

The general spend limit manager algorithm adjusts the bid according to the agent's capacity and it is shown in Algorithm 4, while corresponding parameter values are listed in Table 4. In the first five days of the game the limit is fixed and determined based on the agent's capacity. After analysing the results of the controlled experiment we have concluded that the lack of spend limit has the most significant (negative) impact on CrocodileAgent's profit when its capacity is low.

Query Spend Limit. The query spend limit manager defines a distribution of agent's investments in order to maximize its profit and ensures that the maximum number of clicks for a certain ad is limited in accordance with its predicted quality. The spend limits for the first two days are fixed and they are calculated based on the matching of the CrocodileAgent's specialties with the keywords in a query. In the remainder of the game the spend limit is defined according to the click and conversion ratio, as well as earlier profits. The low ratio corresponds with the successful advertisement.

Algorithm 4. General spend limit manager

if *first five days* **then**
    switch *capacity* **do**
        case *low*
            spend limit = *spend limit low fixed*;
        case *medium*
            spend limit = *spend limit medium fixed*;
        case *high*
            spend limit = *spend limit high fixed*;
    endsw
else
    switch *capacity* **do**
        case *low*
            spend limit = *spend limit low*;
        case *medium*
            spend limit = *min*(*spend limit medium, custom profit*);
        case *high*
            spend limit = *min*(*spend limit high, custom profit*);
    endsw
end

Table 4. Values of parameters for general spend limit

Parameter	Min	Parameter	Min
spend limit low fixed	700	spend limit medium fixed	1000
spend limit high fixed	1200	spend limit low	750
spend limit medium	1150	spend limit high	1350

Table 5. Values of parameters for general spend limit

Parameter	Value	Parameter	Value	Parameter	Value	Parameter	Value
a	60	b	80	ratio lower bound	5	neutral	1.10
c	100	d	120	ratio middle value	10	neutral-hit	1.20
e	140	f	180	minimum limit	20	hit	1.30
				default limit	40		

Therefore, the lower the ratio is, the higher the limit will be. The query spend limit manager algorithm is shown in Algorithm 5, while the corresponding parameter values are listed in Table 5.

Algorithm 5. Query spend limit manager

---

n_{click} = average number of clicks per day;
$n_{conversion}$ = average number of conversions per day;
$mod = n_{click}/n_{conversion}$;
$result$ = a match between query and agent's specialties;
if *first two days* **then**
    switch *result* **do**
        case *miss*
            $limit = a$;
        case *miss-neutral*
            $limit = b$;
        case *miss-hit*
            $limit = c$;
        case *neutral*
            $limit = d$;
        case *neutral-hit*
            $limit = e$;
        case *hit*
            $limit = f$;
    endsw
else
    if $mod < ratio\ lower\ bound$ **then**
        limit = min (minimum limit, revenue/2);
    else if $ratio\ lower\ bound \leq mod \leq ratio\ middle\ value$ **then**
        limit = min (minimum limit, revenue/3);
    else
        limit = default limi;
    end
    limit = `SpecialtyMatchingLimit` (*result, limit*)
end

function `SpecialtyMatchingLimit` (*result, limit*)

switch *result* **do**
    case *neutral*
        $limit = neutral \cdot limit$;
    case *neutral-hit*
        $limit = neutral - hit \cdot limit$;
    case *hit*
        $hit : limit = hit \cdot limit$;
endsw

---

5   Controlled Experiment

In order to evaluate the performance of the CrocodileAgent, which placed 6th in the TAC/AA 2010 Competition Finals, an experiment was conducted by repeating games taking into consideration a fer distribution of agent capacity. Based on the analysis of the results, the CrocodileAgent's deficiencies were identified and guidelines for future improvements were set.

The participants in the experiment were the following agents which competed in the TAC/AA 2010 Competition: *TacTex, Mertacor, Schlemazl, CrocodileAgent, tauagent, EPFLAgent*. Additionally, due to the lack of TAC/AA 2010 agents in the official agent repository[8], two agents from TAC/AA 2009 Competition, *AstonTAC* and *WayneAd*, were included in the experiment. The controlled experiment consisted of 40 games whose average results are shown in Table 6.

Table 6. Average results in the conducted competition

Position	Agent	Game score
1.	TacTex	57 848
2.	Mertacor	53 998
3.	Schlemazl	53 933
4.	CrocodileAgent	49 435
5.	tauagent	47 789
6.	AstonTAC	45 104
7.	EPFLAgent	44 179
8.	WayneAd	36 456

The games in the controlled experiment were configured to ensure fair capacity distribution among competing agents so each agent played ten games with high capacity, twenty games with medium capacity and ten games with low capacity. In each game, two agents had low capacity, two agents had high capacity and four of them had medium capacity. The goal of the experiment was to observe agents' behaviour in respect with the assigned capacities. The results of these observations are shown in Figure 2.

In the graph shown on Figure 2 the bars represent the ratio between the average result of a single agent in those games where the specified capacity (i.e., high, medium or low) was assigned to it and the average result of the same agent in all games. We call this ratio the intra-agent relative profitability. On the other hand, the horizontal lines represent the ratio between average results of all agents in those games where the specified capacity (i.e., high, medium and low) was assigned to them and the average results of all agents in all games. This measure represents the average intra-agent relative profitability of all agents. Finally, squares, triangles and diamonds represent the ratio between the average result of a single agent in those games where the specified capacity (i.e., high, medium or low) was assigned to it and the average result of all agents in those games where the same capacity was assigned to them. This graph enables the comparison of the single agent's average profit achieved in those games where different capacities were assigned to it with: i) its average profit in all games, and, ii) the average profit of all agents in the games where the same capacity was assigned to them. While the former measure enables us to compare the profitability of agent's strategies in those games where different capacities were assigned to it with the agent's overall profitability, the latter measure provides relative benchmarking among different agents.

---

[8] http://www.sics.se/tac/showagents.php

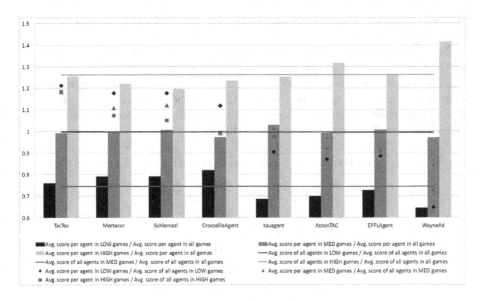

Fig. 2. Agents' relative profit with respect to assigned capacity

If we take a look at the average values of profits achieved in the games with the assigned low capacity, we can notice that the CrocodileAgent has the highest intra-agent relative profitability among all agents in the controlled experiment. However, the CrocodileAgent has smaller intra-agent relative profitability than the average intra-agent relative profitability of all agents in the games where medium and high capacity were assigned to it. At the same time, we can also notice that, when comparing the average score of different agents, the CrocodileAgent has a 12% better score than all agents' average in the games where low capacity was assigned to them, while its performance in both medium and high capacity games is equal to all agents' average in those games.

From this analysis we can identify certain CrocodileAgent's deficiencies. The improvement of those drawbacks in future versions could significantly increase its profits. Namely, we can conclude that the CrocodileAgent should examine the possibility of using other strategies in the games when the agent is assigned with medium or high capacity in order to increase its profit in those games.

Another interesting thing we can learn from Figure 2 is that the relative intra-agent profitability of the TacTex agent, the best agent in the competition, is approximately equal to the average intra-agent profitability of all competing agents (for all three capacity allocations). Furthermore, it is attention-grabbing that the WayneAd agent, who placed last in the competition, has the highest relative intra-agent profitability in those games where the high capacity was assigned to it. However, WayneAd's weakest absolute results in medium and low capacity games are the reason for it placing last in the competition.

After analysing the impact of the assigned capacity on agents' achieved profits, we have also analysed the correlation of the achieved profit and the query category. As mentioned earlier, there are three types of queries (i.e., F0, F1 and F2) that users

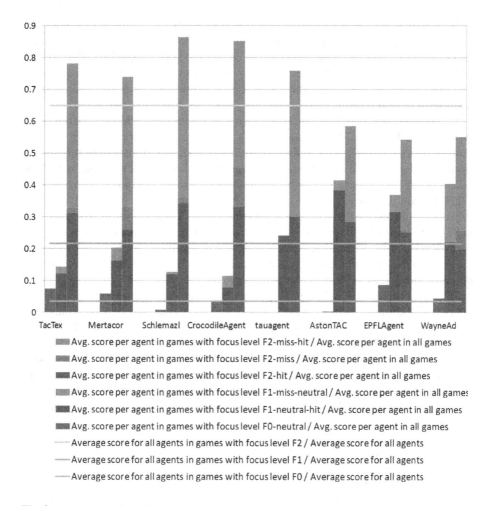

Fig. 3. Distribution of profit achieved from transactions originating from different query classes

generate. Each advertiser selects an ad for display for each query type, choosing between a generic or targeted ad which mentions a particular product [11]. The agents'
profits from all games in the controlled experiment were grouped based on the type of
user query from which the transaction originated from. The mentioned distribution of
agents' profits is presented in Figure 3.

In the graph shown on Figure 3, the horizontal lines represent the ratio between
average results of all agents achieved from transactions originating from queries of the
specified type (i.e., F0, F1 and F2) and the average results of all agents for all types
of queries. On the other hand, the bars represent the ratio between the agent's average
result achieved from transactions originating from queries of the specified type (i.e., F0,
F1 and F2) and the agent's average result achieved from transactions originating from
all types of queries.

If we look at the average values of profits originating from different query types, we can notice that agents, who placed higher in the competition, also achieve higher profits on targeted ads. The last three agents in the competition (i.e., AstonTAC, EPFLAgent and WayneAd) achieved the lowest relative profits from transactions originating from focus level F2 queries and the highest relative profits from transactions originating from focus level F1 queries.

Expressed in percentages and in correlation with the average results for queries of all types, the TacTex made 78% of its total profit from transactions originating from focus level F2 queries and only 22% of its total profit was made from transactions originating from focus level F0 and focus level F1 queries. Agent Schlemazl, who has the highest relative score for transactions originating from focus level F2 queries, achieved 86% of its total profit from those transactions.

Another interesting thing we can learn from Figure 3 is that overall profits are not highly correlated with the fraction of clicks received under manufacturer specialty (i.e., focus level F2-hit). Therefore, we can conclude that shifting spend towards queries focusing on manufacturer speciality is not a guarantee of greater profitability for agents, despite bonuses they get if such transactions take place.

If we analyse the CrocodileAgent's profit distribution depending on the type of user query that the transactions originated from, we can notice that the CrocodileAgent achieves approximately 85% of its total profit from transactions originating from focus level F2 queries. This percentage is higher for the CrocodileAgent than for two leading agents, TacTex and Mertacor. On the other hand, the CrocodileAgent achieved lower relative profits than the TacTex and Mertacor from transactions originating from focus level F1 queries. We can conclude that the CrocodileAgent should try to redistribute a few percent of its profit obtained from F2-queries to F1-queries, while maintaining the share of F0-queries.

6   Conclusion and Future Work

The Trading Agent Competition Ad Auctions (TAC/AA) game enables the academic community and advertising industry to analyse the effects of various bidding strategies by running simulations of sponsored search scenarios. Furthermore, the fact that sponsored search is the most profitable online advertising revenue format also gives great importance to ad auction research.

In this paper, we presented bidding strategies of the CrocodileAgent, the representative of University of Zagreb in the TAC/AA 2010 Tournament. Furthermore, we conducted a controlled experiment with the best-ranked agents from 2010 and 2009 TAC/AA Finals. Based on the analysis of the controlled experiment, we: i) explained some of the reasons why certain agents performed better than others, and, ii) identified CrocodileAgent's behaviours that should be improved in order to boost its performance.

For future work we plan to enhance CrocodileAgent's performance by implementing guidelines for improvements derived from the analysis of the controlled experiment. Namely, we will: i) redesign strategies for achieving profits in the games with assigned medium or high capacity to our agent, and ii) redistribute a part of the relative CrocodileAgent's profit made from transactions originating from focus level F2 queries to transactions originating from focus level F1 queries.

Acknowledgments. The authors acknowledge the support of research project "Content Delivery and Mobility of Users and Services in New Generation Networks" (036-0362027-1639), funded by the Ministry of Science, Education and Sports of the Republic of Croatia.

References

1. Feng, J., Bhargava, H.K., Pennock, D.M.: Implementing sponsored search in web search engines: Computational evaluation of alternative mechanisms. INFORMS Journal on Computing 19(1), 137–148 (2007)
2. Chen, J., Feng, J., Whinston, A.B.: Keyword auctions, unit-price contracts, and the role of commitment. Production and Operations Management 19(3), 305–321 (2010)
3. Easley, D., Kleinberg, J.: Networks, Crowds, and Markets: Reasoning About a Highly Connected World. Cambridge University Press (2010)
4. Joachims, T., Granka, L., Pan, B., Hembrooke, H., Gay, G.: Accurately interpreting click-through data as implicit feedback. In: Proceedings of the 28th ACM SIGIR Conference on Research and Development in Information Retrieval, SIGIR 2005, pp. 154–161. ACM, New York (2005)
5. Craswell, N., Zoeter, O., Taylor, M., Ramsey, B.: An experimental comparison of click position-bias models. In: Proceedings of the International Conference on Web Search and Web Data Mining, WSDM 2008, pp. 87–94. ACM, New York (2008)
6. Jeziorski, P., Segal, I.: What makes them click: Empirical analysis of consumer demand for search advertising. Economics Working Paper Archive 569, The Johns Hopkins University, Department of Economics (2010)
7. Lahaie, S.: An analysis of alternative slot auction designs for sponsored search. In: Proceedings of the 7th ACM Conference on Electronic Commerce, EC 2006, pp. 218–227. ACM, New York (2006)
8. Lahaie, S., Parkes, D.C., Pennock, D.M.: An expressive auction design for online display advertising. In: Proceedings of the 23rd National Conference on Artificial Intelligence, vol. 1, pp. 108–113. AAAI Press (2008)
9. Varian, H.R.: Online ad auctions. American Economic Review 99(2), 430–434 (2009)
10. Acharya, S., Krishnamurthy, P., Deshpande, K., Yan, T., Chang, C.C.: A Simulation Framework for Evaluating Designs for Sponsored Search Markets. In: 16th International World Wide Web Conference (2007)
11. Jordan, P.R., Cassell, B., Callender, L.F., Wellman, M.P.: The ad auctions game for the 2009 trading agent competition. Technical report (2009)
12. Jordan, P.R., Wellman, M.P.: Designing an Ad Auctions Game for the Trading Agent Competition. In: David, E., Gerding, E., Sarne, D., Shehory, O. (eds.) AMEC/TADA 2009. LNBIP, vol. 59, pp. 147–162. Springer, Heidelberg (2010)
13. Arunachalam, R., Sadeh, N.M.: The supply chain trading agent competition. Electronic Commerce Research and Applications 4(1), 66–84 (2005)
14. Podobnik, V., Petric, A., Jezic, G.: An Agent-Based Solution for Dynamic Supply Chain Management. Journal of Universal Computer Science 14(7), 1080–1104 (2008)
15. Sardinha, A., Benisch, M., Sadeh, N., Ravichandran, R., Podobnik, V., Stan, M.: The 2007 procurement challenge: A competition to evaluate mixed procurement strategies. Electronic Commerce Research and Applications 8(2), 106–114 (2009)
16. Niu, J., Cai, K., Parsons, S., Gerding, E., McBurney, P.: Characterizing effective auction mechanisms: insights from the 2007 TAC market design competition. In: Proceedings of the 7th International Joint Conference on Autonomous Agents and Multiagent Systems, AAMAS 2008, pp. 1079–1086. International Foundation for Autonomous Agents and Multiagent Systems (2008)

17. Petric, A., Podobnik, V., Grguric, A., Zemljic, M.: Designing an Effective E-Market: An Overview of the CAT Agent. In: Proceedings of AAAI 2008 Workshop on Trading Agent Design and Analysis, TADA 2008, pp. 62–65. AAAI Press (2008)
18. Block, C., Collins, J., Ketter, W.: Agent-based competitive simulation: Exploring future retail energy markets. In: Twelfth International Conference on Electronic Commerce (ICEC 2010), pp. 67–76. ACM (2010)
19. Lahaie, S., Pennock, D.M.: Revenue analysis of a family of ranking rules for keyword auctions. In: Proceedings of the 8th ACM Conference on Electronic Commerce, EC 2007, pp. 50–56. ACM, New York (2007)
20. Berg, J., Greenwald, A., Naroditskiy, V., Sodomka, E.: A first approach to autonomous bidding in ad auctions. In: EC 2010 Workshop on Trading Agent Design and Analysis, TADA 2010. ACM, New York (2010)
21. Pardoe, D., Stone, P.: A particle filter for bid estimation in ad auctions with periodic ranking observations. In: EC 2010 Workshop on Trading Agent Design and Analysis, TADA 2010. ACM, Cambridge (2010)
22. Cigler, L.: Semester project: Bidding agent for advertisement auctions. Technical report, Ecole Polytechnique Federale de Lausanne (2009)
23. Witten, I.H., Frank, E.: Data Mining: Practical Machine Learning Tools and Techniques. Morgan Kaufmann Publishers, San Francisco (2005)

Dealing with Trust and Reputation in Unreliable Multi-agent Trading Environments

Iraklis Tsekourakis and Andreas L. Symeonidis

Electrical and Computer Engineering Department, Aristotle University
of Thessaloniki Thessaloniki, Greece
htsekourakis@gmail.com, asymeon@eng.auth.gr

Abstract. In shared competitive environments, where information comes from various sources, agents may interact with each other in a competitive manner in order to achieve their individual goals. Numerous research efforts exist, attempting to define protocols, rules and interfaces for agents to abide by and ensure trustworthy exchange of information. Auction environments and e-commerce platforms are such paradigms, where trust and reputation are vital factors determining agent strategy. And though the process is always secured with a number of safeguards, there is always the issue of unreliability. In this context, the Agent Reputation and Trust (ART) testbed has provided researchers with the ability to test different trust and reputation strategies, in various types of trust/reputation environments. Current work attempts to identify the most viable trust and reputation models stated in the literature, while it further elaborates on the issue by proposing a robust trust and reputation mechanism. This mechanism is incorporated in our agent, HerculAgent, and tested in a variety of environments against the top performing agents of the ART competition. The paper provides a thorough analysis of ART, presents HerculAgent s architecture and dis-cuss its performance.

1 Introduction

Agent Technology (AT) is constantly gaining ground in domains where continuous interaction is required. Software Agents may act in uncertain and dynamic environments, adapt illustrating various levels of autonomy and collaborate or compete in order to achieve their goals. Examples of such dynamic domains are Peer to Peer (P2P) networks, e-business and m-commerce solutions, autonomic and grid computing, as well as pervasive computing environments. [1]

It is more than obvious that interaction may entail malice, with agents (human or software) aiming to promote own interest while at the same time disserving others. In order to deal with this problem, the concepts of *trust* and *reputation* (T&R) are employed, providing agents with useful insight on which agents to trust and interact with.

Current work aims to analyze and discuss existing approaches on trust and reputation. Analysis is performed against the Agent Reputation and Trust testbed,

E. David et al. (Eds.): AMEC/TADA 2011, LNBIP 119, pp. 87–101, 2013.
© Springer-Verlag Berlin Heidelberg 2013

a multi-parametric environment designed and developed for testing various trust strategies. Based on the analysis performed, a trust and reputation mechanism is developed and embedded into *HerculAgent* that is benchmarked against the top scoring agents of the ART competition. The paper is organized as follows: Section 2 discusses state-of-the-art on the available trust and reputation models, while Section 3 provides an overview of ART, discusses the winning T&R strategies and performs a preliminary analysis in order to identify the key factors affecting performance. Section 4 introduces the proposed T&R model and outlines the *HerculAgent* architecture. Finally, Section 5 discusses the performance of the agent on a set of experiments, while Section 6 proposes future directions and concludes the paper.

2   Trust and Reputation Models

There exists extensive literature related to trust and reputation, since it is strongly related to the application domain and the technologies used. Nevertheless, all approaches share a set of common factors, which are discussed within the context of this Section. Additionally, one should keep in mind that current work is focused on the T&R aspects in multi-agent trading environments, thus emphasis is given in that direction.

2.1   Specifying Trust and Reputation

Trust is the fundamental concern in open distributed systems. It lies at the core of all interactions between the entities that have to operate in uncertain and constantly changing environments. [2] In case of open multi-agent trading environments, trust pervades multi-agent interactions at all levels. In general, trust models are useful in spotting and marginalizing unreliable/malicious agents, in evaluating the outcome of an interaction and in leading to decisions on trustworthy agents to transact with.

Trust may be conceptualized in the following ways:

- **Individual-level trust**, whereby an agent has a set of beliefs about the honesty or reciprocate nature of the agents it interacts with;
- **System-level trust**, whereby agents operating in an environment are forced to be trustworthy by the rules of encounter (i.e. protocols and mechanisms) that regulate the system.

Should one discuss trust in the broader context where agents may act according to self-interest, and given that system-level trust mechanisms take a *de facto* approach on agent honesty, it is evident that individual-level trust issues are of great importance in contemporary trading environments. Research literature proposes three main approaches for specifying trust: the use of *A priori* evidence, the use of *Experienced* evidence, and the use of *Reputation*.

***A Priori* Evidence.** *A priori* evidence is evidence provided by specific protocols, policies and mechanisms which guarantee trust between participants. [3] In other words, when an agent acts following the rules that the protocols, policies, or mechanisms dictate ensures that this agent can be trusted.

***Experienced* Evidence.** As its name implies, experienced evidence is retrieved by agent interactions. This category is classified into two sub-categories: *direct* experience evidence [4] and *witness* evidence. [5]

Direct experience is the most relevant and reliable evidence source for trust management. It is the information an agent gains through the direct interactions with its partners. The trust reasoning efficiency of an agent is proportionate to the size of the interaction history saved by the agent. It is, though, disproportionate to the evidential effectiveness.

Witness evidence originates from the interactions of other agents in the community, which in turn may come from direct experience or witness evidence. Thus, the accuracy of evidence is strongly related to the source of evidence; due to its uncertainty, witness evidence is rarely exploited in existing trading environments.

Reputation Management. Reputation is the most exploited concept in trust management of multi-agent systems. Though the definition of reputation varies with respect to the context of the domain it is applied, one could argue that reputation is expressed as three levels of rating that may express the trustworthiness of an agent against other agents: *individual ratings, collective ratings* and the *rating transmissions*. In terms of rating, the techniques that manage the ratings could be divided to *rating retrieval* techniques, and *rating aggregation* techniques.

Rating retrieval is applied on distributed trading environments, where the topology is not known beforehand and network analysis techniques are employed in order to retrieve ratings.[6] [7] Having retrieved ratings, rating aggregation is performed in order to calculate reputation and define trust. In literature, rating aggregation may be performed in a number of manners, ranging from naive to more sophisticated ones.

2.2   Efficiency of Trust and Reputation Models

A successful trust and reputation model depends on the type of evidence the model provides to agents, the techniques used to get the above evidence, and the way an agent handles such evidence to extract trustworthiness for others. Efficiency of a T&R model is defined with respect to the following axes [8]:

- *Accuracy.* T&R models must provide good prediction on another agents future behavior. [9]
- *Adaptivity.* T&R models must be able to adapt in order to accommodate dynamic trustworthiness characteristics of other agents. [10]

- *Quick Convergence.* T&R modeling algorithms must quickly generate new models when unknown agents enter the system. [11]
- *Multidimensionality.* T&R models must differentiate between another agents varied trustworthiness characteristics across multiple categories. [12]
- *Efficiency.* T&R algorithms must generate models with minimal computational cost and in minimal time.

3   The ART Testbed

3.1   The ART Scenario and Architecture

As already discussed, a variety of approaches exist, aiming to model trust and reputation in multi-agent systems. The Agent Reputation and Trust (ART) testbed [13] provides an ideal framework for benchmarking different T&R strategies.

Within the context of ART, each agent represent an art appraiser, competing against all other agents (appraisers) in the system. Clients (handled by the ART server) request appraisals for paintings from different eras. In case an appraiser is an expert on paintings of the specific era, it is capable for providing an accurate appraisal, thus satisfying the client that will buy the painting and pay the appraiser. In case the agent is not an expert on paintings of the era, it may request paying a fee an evaluation (defined as opinion) by other appraisers. Appraisers may also transact with each other on reputation information on other appraisers. Based on their T&R strategy, agents must decide when and from whom to request opinions and reputation information, in order to generate accurate appraisals for clients. The more accurate the appraisals, the more the clients attracted and profit for the appraiser. Winner agent is declared the one with the highest bank account balance. Figure 1 illustrates the possible interactions and the type of information ex-changed between appraisers and clients. More information on ART can be found at [13].

The ART testbed comprises four basic modules [14]:

- *The Simulation Engine,* which is responsible for generat-ing controlled T&R environments by enforcing user-defined parameters.
- *The ART Database,* which stores all game information for reporting and later retrieval.
- *The ART GUI,* providing access to online game monitor-ing and result visualization.
- *The Agent Skeleton,* an agent wrapper for researchers to embed their T&R strategy, while ensuring unflustered communication with the other ART entities.

3.2   ART T&R Modeling and State-of-the-Art

Within the context of ART, an agent T&R strategy should span across three axes: (i) modeling of the other agents (environment), (ii) modeling request and,

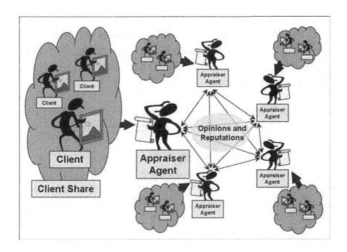

Fig. 1. ART entities and their interactions

(iii) modeling response. The response strategy directly affects its reputation, while the request and response strategies have an effect on environment modeling. [15]

The basic challenges in building an efficient T&R strategy have been identified by Costa et al. [2008] [16] and are: (i) the start game opinion requests, (ii) the identification of trustworthy agents, (iii) the appraisal definition policy and complexity, (iv) the reputation definition, request and response policies and, finally, the aggregation of all the above. Researchers may focus on one or more aspects of the strategy, in order to build an efficient agent.

May one go through related literature, one may identify several approaches that perform ART T&R modeling. Nevertheless, two are the ones that stand out: UNO and IAM.

UNO. Probably the most successful and efficient ART T&R model. Murillo and Munoz [17] focused on the request and response aspects of the T&R model. In both cases they exploit knowledge the agent builds on the other agents, based on:

– the error of own appraisals
– if an agent has responded to an UNO request and,
– the total number of requests an agent has made to UNO.

It is worth mentioning that UNO does not employ a reputation mechanism to extract trust values, since the UNO team considered that the number of participating agents is too small for generating trustworthy reputation estimations. Thus, they selected to work directly with the real appraisal error of each agent.

IAM. IAM is another successful ART agent paradigm. Teacy et al [18] describe IAM behavior as *Intelligent* (using statistic-al models for opponent modeling), *Abstemious* (spending its budget parsimoniously based on its trust model) and *Moral* (providing fair and honest feedback to those that request it). IAM decides based on the following information:

- Appraisal responses from the Simulator Engine and other appraisers
- Information on the behavior of other agents (e.g. reputation values).

The trust model of IAM comprises three parts: (a) the *lie detector*, which identifies malicious agents, (b) the *variation appraiser*, which estimates the variation of appraisal errors of the other agents and (c) the *weight estimator of the most accurate agents*. In contrast to UNO, IAM employs reputation in order to build its T&R model.

3.3   Preliminary Analysis of the ART Environment

In order to identify the factors that mostly affect appraiser performance, we performed an extensive set of experiments, where different game parameters and simple policies were tested. We employed the SimpleAgent (provided by the ART framework) and gradually tested it against the TestAgent (SimpleAgent equipped with a simple policy), the Cheatin-gAgent and HonestAgent, as well as the agents that participated in the 2008 ART competition. In the latter experiments, more elaborate policies where followed, based on the analysis performed. In all cases the game parameters were the same; these are defined in Table 1.

Table 1. Game parameters during experimentation

Time Epochs	50
Eras	10
Average number of clients per appraiser	20
Client fee	100
Appraisal cost	10
Certainty cost	1
Reputation cost	0.1
Appraisal messages	2
Certainty messages	20
Denial of personal opinion	True
Variable eras	2
Expertise value change	0.05

The types of policies investigated are discussed in Ta-ble 2, where the last column defines the number of discrete steps selected for each of the T&R factors. It should be mentioned that the following results are aggregates following monte carlo analysis.

Table 2. The various policies applied

Policy	T&R factor	Steps
Pol-1	Reputation definition policy	7
Pol-2	Reputation request policy (reputation only)	5
Pol-3	Reputation response policy	3
Pol-4	Honesty policy (based on agent trustworthiness)	3
Pol-5	Reputation request policy (reputation and certainty)	3
Pol-6	Appraisal cost for trustworthy agents	5
Pol-7	Appraisal cost for unreliable agents	5
Pol-8	Trustworthiness with respect to appraisal cost	3
Pol-9	Optimal reputation definition policy (Pol-1)	4
	Optimal trustworthiness policy (Pol-4)	
	Honest response to trustworthy agents	
	Dishonest response to unreliable agents	
Pol-10	Optimal reputation definition policy (Pol-1)	3
	Honest response to trustworthy agents	
	Dishonest response to unreliable agents	
	Optimal appraisal cost policy (Pol-6)	
Pol-11	Optimal reputation definition policy (Pol-1)	3
	Optimal reputation response policy (Pol-3)	
	Optimal appraisal cost policy (Pol-6)	
	Honest response to trustworthy agents	
	Dishonest response to unreliable agents	
Pol-12	Optimal reputation definition policy (Pol-1)	3
	Optimal reputation response policy (Pol-3)	
	Optimal appraisal cost policy (Pol-6, Pol-7)	
	Honest response to trustworthy agents	
	Dishonest response to unreliable agents	

TestAgent vs. SimpleAgent. An extensive set of tests was performed on the simple policies applied (Pol.1 Pol.8), in order to identify which of the T&R factors affect appraiser performance. Subfigures 2.1 2.8 illustrate the performance of the competing agents in various configurations (omitted due to space limitations). Block 1 denotes the set of basic rules identified and the optimal values of the most important factors:

BLOCK 1. BASIC RULES IDENTIFIED

```
Rule-1. IF ME > 0.5 THEN rep = rep-0.02 ELSE rep = rep+0.04
Rule-2. IF repAppraiser > 0.5 THEN it is considered trustworthy
Rule-3. IF an appraiser is trustworthy
        THEN provide accurate opinions
        ELSE provide falsified opinions
Rule-4. IF an appraiser is trustworthy
        THEN pay 0,7*AppCost to get an appraisal
        ELSE pay 0,15*AppCost
```

TestAgent vs. HonestAgent and CheatingAgent. The ART testbed provides two more agents for benchmarking: the *CheatingAgent* and *HonestAgent*. *TestAgent* equipped with the knowledge base generated during the first experimentation stage (Pol.1 Pol.8), was benchmarked against these agents. Subfigures 2.9 2.11 illustrate the performance of the competing agents in various configurations. Apart all other observations, one should also point out that in some cases, *SimpleAgent* stills outperforms *TestAgent*, since the strategy the latter follows is oriented towards more complex strategies.

TestAgent vs. ART 2008 Winning Agents. Finally, *TestAgent* was benchmarked against the top per-forming agents of the ART 2008 competition. Subfigure 2.12 illustrates the performance of the competing agents in various configurations. At this point *TestAgent* outperforms *SimpleAgent*, since the latter cannot cope with the complexity of the competitors strategies. Nevertheless, it is obvious that the approach *TestAgent* follows still lacks dynamicity and adjustability.

A number of useful observations were made through the analysis performed. First of all, computing reputation based on direct interactions with other agents proved more efficient than using information from reputation responses. Additionally, experimentation dictated that neither honesty, nor unreliability work alone. Competitors should be forced to play fair, so as to be rewarded with trust (or penalized with unreliability). Finally, the ranges of metric values were identified, where our agent increased efficiency. Outside of these ranges agent performance decreases. Based on these observations, *HerculAgent* was developed.

4   *HerculAgent* Architecture

HerculAgent follows a modular architecture, so as to meet each of the diverse needs imposed by the ART framework (Figure 3). Its behavior is expressed through nine strategy functions, which are aggregated into three behavior modules implementing three protocols: the *reputation protocol*, the *certainty protocol* and the *opinion protocol*.

4.1   *HerculAgent* Protocols

Reputation Protocol. The reputation protocol manages the reputation values $Rep_i jt$(i: $Agent_i$,, j: Era_j, t: $Epoch_t$), primarily based on previous direct interactions, and secondarily on indirect sources such as observation information. The *reputation* module actually deliberates on the reward or admonition strategy to follow, based on the appraisal estimates provided by other appraisers in the past. It also defines the number of reputation re-quests *HerculAgent* will make and the agents to request reputation information from. Finally, the *reputation* module determines the response strategy to reputation requests the agent receives from other agents.

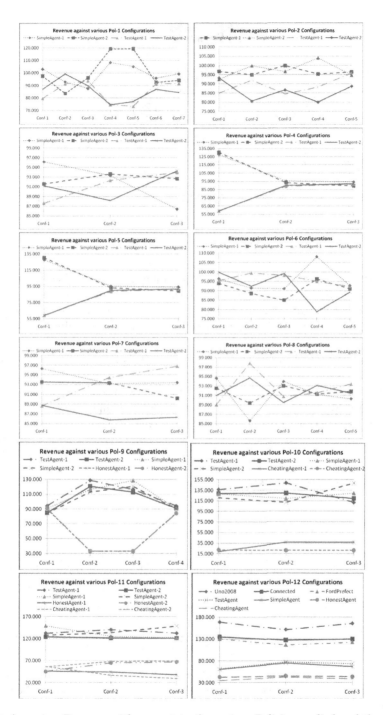

Fig. 2. Appraiser Revenue with respect to the various Policies applied and the configuration settings selected

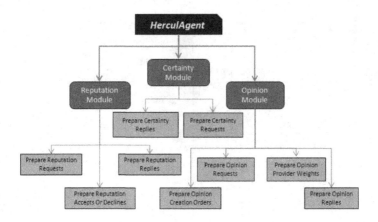

Fig. 3. The HerculAgent architecture

Certainty Protocol. The certainty protocol manages the certainty values Cer_ijt (i: $Agent_i$,, j: Era_j, t: $Epoch_t$) and refers to the confidence an agent has on the reputation of other appraisers. The *certainty* module implements the strategy *HerculAgent* has with respect to which agents to ask for their certainty values.

Opinion Protocol. Finally, the opinion protocol is the core business protocol of the agent, responsible for issuing accurate painting appraisals/opinions. The *opinion* module selects the agents to trust and request their opinion, while it also builds its own personal opinions base to respond to competition agents. It contemplates the strategy that the agent uses to define the combination of the other agents appraisals to create its own final appraisal and finally send it to the client.

4.2 *HerculAgent* Metrics

HerculAgent employs four metrics in order to design and develop its T&R strategy:

Mean error (ME(i,j,t)) is the weighted average of the appraisal relative errors an agent makes and varies for each era. ME depends on past interactions and is defined as:

$$ME(i,j,t) = \frac{((ME(i,j,t-1) * ErC(i,j,t-1) + Er(i,j,t-1)))}{(ErC(i,j,t-1) + 1)} \quad (1)$$

where Er(i,j,t), is the relative appraisal error $Agent_i$, makes for a painting of Era_j at $Epoch_t$ of the game. ErC(i,j,t) is the respective number of the errors.

Reputation (Rep(i,j,t)) expresses the level of trustworthiness of $Agent_i$, for a painting of Era_j at $Epoch_t$ of the game. It ranges in the [0,1] interval.

Certainty (Cer(i,j,t)) indicates the certainty that an *Agent$_i$* claims on its appraisal values for a painting of *Era$_j$* at epoch *Epoch$_t$* of the game. It ranges in the $[0,1]$ interval.

Self Confidence (SC(i,j,t)) expresses the certainty *HerculAgent* has on the other appraiser agents, as defined through past interactions. It denotes the possibility that the Rep(i,j,t) value computed for an appraiser is similar to its Cer(i,j,t) value. Block-2 denotes the pseudocode implementation of SC:

BLOCK 2. calculates() PSEUDOCODE

```
FUNCTION calculateSC(Agent i, Era j, Epoch t){
L1:   tempConf <- selfConfidence(Agenti(Appraisal(Eraj)));
L2:   IF (tempConf EQUALS 0) THEN tempConf = a
      ELSE tempConf = tempConf+((1-tempConf)*b);   {1}
L3:   selfConfidence(Agent_{i}(Appraisal(Era_{j}))) <- tempConf;
}
{1} After experimentation, a = 0.01, b = 0.005
```

Metrics are continuously calculated for each agent, era and epoch.

4.3 Dynamic Behavior Adaptation

HerculAgent employs two methods in order to adapt its behavior and strategy with respect to the data collected throughout the game:

setRepLimit() which adapts, for each *Agent$_i$*, for paintings of *Era$_j$* at each *Epoch$_t$* the minimum Rep(i,j,t) value *Agent$_i$* has to meet to be trusted.

setErrorsLimit() which defines, for each *Agent$_i$*, for paintings of *Era$_j$* at each *Epoch$_t$* the error limit that is acceptable for an appraiser agent.

Block-3 denotes the pseudocode implementation of *setErrorsLimit()*. Function *setRepLimit()* is deployed in a similar manner.

BLOCK 3. setErrorsLimit() PSEUDOCODE

```
FUNCTION setErrorsLimit(Agent i, Era j, Epoch t){
L1:   FOR (1 TO numberOfEras){
L2:      min <- 1;
L3:      max <- 0;
L4:      FOR (1 TO numberOfAgents){
L5:         IF (errors(Agent_{i}, Era_{j}) < min
L6:         THEN min <- errors(Agent_{i}, Era_{j});
L7:         IF errors(Agent_{i}, Era_{j})> max
L8:         THEN max <- errors(Agent_{i}, Era_{j});
      }
L9:   ErrrorsLimit <- min + *max^2;   {1}
      }
}
{1} After experimentation,  = 0.2
```

4.4 *HerculAgent* Behavior

The core T&R model of *HerculAgent* focuses on trust, and the degree of trust-worthiness we show to opponents. In order to decide, three behaviors were implemented: (i) the *typical* behavior (our basic strategy), (ii) the *optimistic behavior*, where opponents are given more credit and, (iii) the *pessimistic* behavior, where opponents are given less credit. In a similar manner, three behaviors were implemented in order to calculate the weighted average of the final appraisal: the *typical, aggressive*, and *submissive* behaviors. All behaviors are specified in the respective *HerculAgent.conf* file and behavior changes dynamically (upon game initiation).

5   Experiments

A number of experiments were performed with *HerculAgent* participating in all agent scenarios, as defined in Section 3. Various strategies were applied and interesting conclusions were drawn. The following results are aggregates following monte carlo analysis.

At first, *HerculAgent* was tested against the nave set of agents that were tested in the preliminary phase, and easily outperformed them. Figure 4 illustrates agent revenue (Bank balance) of an indicative game, as depicted by the ART Light Game Monitor Interface.

Consequently, *HerculAgent* was tested against the top performing agents of the ART 2008 competition. Figure 5 illustrates agent revenue (Bank balance) of an indicative game, while Figure 6 presents the aggregate results with respect to the different *HerculAgent* behaviors.

Through the numerous experiments performed in order to compare our strategy against the winning agents of the ART 2008 competition, we observe that our results are satisfactory but could be further improved. *HerculAgent* often succeeded in finished second third, nevertheless never succeeded in beating *Uno*.

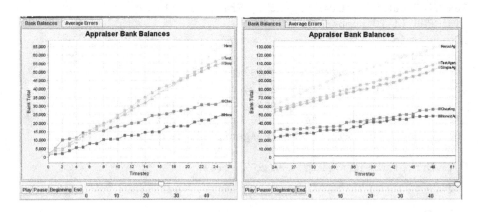

Fig. 4. HerculAgent against the naive set of agents

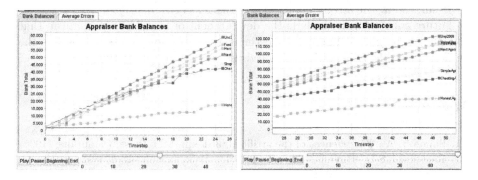

Fig. 5. HerculAgent against the ART 2008 top performing agents

The strategy of *HerculAgent* did not perform adequately at the first half of the game (start game effect). This can be justified based on the fact that *HerculAgent* computes trust mainly on information received through direct interactions. Thus, during the initial epochs there is not enough information available for reasoning. Whenever accurate initial appraisals are performed, the agent performs very well. In all cases, though, in the second half of the game, the bank total of *HerculAgent* improves significantly, at a rate even greater than the winner agent *Uno*.

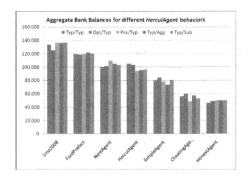

Fig. 6. Aggregate performance of HerculAgent against the ART 2008 top performing agents

6   Conclusions - Future Work

Current work discusses *HerculAgent*, an agent designed and developed for the analysis of various T&R models in dynamic trading environments. The ART platform was selected for experimentation, given that it provides a unique testbed for testing various game parameters. Preliminary analysis indicated the basic factors affecting performance, and a set of rules of thumb were identified, which where later embedded in our agent model.

Results show the strong points and drawbacks of *HerculAgent*.

Future enhancements include the development of an off-line mechanism that exploits regression techniques for estimating reputation values, as well as the improvement of the agent behavior during the first epochs of the game.

References

1. Simon, H.A.: The sciences of the artificial, 3rd edn. MIT Press, Cambridge (1996)
2. Ramchurn, S.D., Huynh, D., Jennings, N.R.: Trust in multi-agent systems. Knowl. Eng. Rev. 19, 1–25 (2004)
3. Huang, H., Zhu, G., Jin, S.: Revisiting trust and reputation in multi-agent systems. In: ISECS International Colloquium on Computing, Communication, Control and Management, vol. 1, pp. 424–429 (2008)
4. Ramchurn, S.D., Sierra, C., Godo, L., Jennings, N.R.: A computational trust model for multi-agent interactions based on confidence and reputation. In: Proceedings of 6th International Workshop of Deception, Fraud and Trust in Agent Societies, pp. 69–75 (2003)
5. Gómez, M., Carbó, J., Benac-Earle, C.: An Anticipatory Trust Model for Open Distributed Systems. In: Butz, M.V., Sigaud, O., Pezzulo, G., Baldassarre, G. (eds.) ABiALS 2006. LNCS (LNAI), vol. 4520, pp. 307–324. Springer, Heidelberg (2007)
6. Fullam, K.K., Barber, K.S.: Learning trust strategies in reputation exchange networks. In: Proceedings of the Fifth International Joint Conference on Autonomous Agents and Multiagent Systems, AAMAS 2006, pp. 1241–1248. ACM, New York (2006)
7. Sabater, J., Sierra, C.: Reputation and social network analysis in multi-agent systems. In: Proceedings of the First International Joint Conference on Autonomous Agents and Multiagent Systems: Part 1, AAMAS 2002, pp. 475–482. ACM, New York (2002)
8. Fullam, K.K., Klos, T.B., Muller, G., Sabater, J., Schlosser, A., Topol, Z., Barber, K.S., Rosenschein, J.S., Vercouter, L., Voss, M.: A specification of the agent reputation and trust (art) testbed: Experimentation and competition for trust in agent societies. In: The Fourth International Joint Conference on Autonomous Agents and Multiagent Systems, Utrecht, The Netherlands, pp. 512–518 (July 2005)
9. Fullam, K.K.: An expressive belief revision framework based on information valuation. Master's thesis, Dept. of EE, U. Texas (Austin) (2003)
10. Fullam, K.K., Barber, K.S.: A Temporal Policy for Trusting Information. In: Falcone, R., Barber, S.K., Sabater-Mir, J., Singh, M.P. (eds.) Trusting Agents. LNCS (LNAI), vol. 3577, pp. 75–94. Springer, Heidelberg (2005)
11. Ding, L., Kolari, P., Ganjugunte, S., Finin, T., Joshi, A.: Modeling and Evaluating Trust Network Inference. In: Seventh International Workshop on Trust in Agent Societies at AAMAS 2004 (July 2004)
12. Muller, G., Vercouter, L., Boissier, O.: Towards a general definition of trust and its application to openness in MAS. In: Falcone, R., Barber, K., Korba, L., Singh, M. (eds.) Proceedings of the Workshop on Deception, Fraud and Trust in Agent Societies at Autonomous Agents and Multi-Agent Systems, pp. 49–56 (July 2003)
13. ART testbed website: http://www.ncbi.nlm.nih.gov/

14. Fullam, K.K., Klos, T., Muller, G., Sabater-Mir, J., Barber, K.S., Vercouter, L.: The Agent Reputation and Trust (ART) Testbed. In: Stølen, K., Winsborough, W.H., Martinelli, F., Massacci, F. (eds.) iTrust 2006. LNCS, vol. 3986, pp. 439–442. Springer, Heidelberg (2006)
15. Kafalı, Ö., Yolum, P.: Trust strategies for ART Testbed. In: Ninth International Workshop on Trust in Agent Societies, AAMAS, pp. 43–49 (2006)
16. da Costa, A.D., de Lucena, C.J.P., da Silva, V.T., Azevedo, S.C., Soares, F.A.: Computing reputation in the art context: Agent design to handle negotiation challenges (2008)
17. Muñoz, V., Murillo, J.: Agent uno: Winner in the 2nd spanish art competition. Inteligencia Artificial, Revista Iberoamericana de Inteligencia Artificial 12(39), 19–27 (2008)
18. Teacy, W.T.L., Huynh, T.D., Dash, R.K., Jennings, N.R., Patel, J., Luck, M.: The art of iam: The winning strategy for the 2006 competition (2006)

Analysis of Stable Prices
in Non-Decreasing Sponsored Search Auction

ChenKun Tsung[1], HannJang Ho[2], and SingLing Lee[1]

[1] Dep. of Computer Science and Information Engineering,
National Chung Cheng University,
168 University Road, Minhsiung, Chiayi 62102, Taiwan, ROC
[2] Dep. of Applied Digital Media,
WuFeng University,
117, Sec 2, Chiankuo Road, Minhsiung, Chiayi 62102, Taiwan, ROC
{tck95p,hjho,singling}@cs.ccu.edu.tw

Abstract. Most critical challenge of applying generalized second price
(GSP) idea in multi-round sponsored search auction (SSA) is to prevent
revenue loss for search engine provider (SEP). In this paper, we propose non-decreasing Sponsored Search Auction (NDSSA) to guarantee
SEP's revenue. Each advertiser's bid increment is restricted by minimum increase price (MIP) in NDSSA. The MIP determination strategy
influences bid convergence speed and SEP's revenue. Fixed MIP strategy and Additive-Increase/Multiplicative-Decrease (AIMD) principle are
applied to determine MIP values, and they are evaluated in this paper.
For the convergence speed analysis, fixed MIP strategy converges faster
than AIME in most instances. For SEP's revenue, AIMD assists SEP
to gain more revenue than fixed MIP strategy by experiments. Simultaneously, SEP's revenue in Vickrey-Clarke-Groves auction (VCG) is the
lower bound of that in AIMD.

Keywords: Sponsored Search Auction, Generalized Second Price Auction, Minimum Increase Price, Additive-Increase/Multiplicative-Decrease,
lower bound.

1 Introduction

Recently, search engine provider (SEP) combines advertising and search results
on the screen. This kind of advertising application is called as sponsored search
auction (SSA).

Many advertisers would like to join SSA due to the pay-per-click design. Only
advertiser whose advertisement is clicked by the Internet user is charged. To
simulate the click event, the click-through-rate (CTR) is introduced [1]. CTR is a
probability that the Internet user clicks on. Thus, the quality of each advertising
slot can be estimated by the CTR assumption.

Aggarwal et al. suggest that the CTR should be evaluated according a
merchant-specific factor and a position-specific factor [9]. So, the relevance of

E. David et al. (Eds.): AMEC/TADA 2011, LNBIP 119, pp. 102–114, 2013.

each advertisement and inputted keywords impacts CTR. For simplification, most related works only consider position-specific factor, such as [1] [2].

Generalized Second price (GSP) [1] is the famous charging function in real world SSA applications. Each clicked advertiser pays equal to the bid value of next ranked advertiser. Comparing to the idea of paying what he/she bids, advertisers in GSP will save more money.

Bu et al. [7] and Cary et al. [6] study the multi-round SSA, while SEP's revenue may be reduced round by round. When an advertiser is benefited in a worse position, he/she will propose a lower bid in the next round. Therefore, SEP's revenue will be decreased because the revenue comes from the sum of payments.

According to [6] [7], we propose Non-decreasing Sponsored Search Auction (NDSSA) to improve SEP's revenue by allowing biding on only non-decreasing prices. Thus, advertisers will compete for better slots to improve utilities, that is similar to English auction, and the revenue loss problem is resolved.

However, SEP suffers an extended issue: long-term revenue loss problem. SEP's long-term revenue is the sum of payments after several rounds. Less payment will also improve advertiser's long-term utility. Either the initial bid with extremely low value is proposed or increasing bid values slightly is beneficial for long-term utility of each advertiser. So, SEP's revenue in each round will be raised slowly, and the long-term revenue loss problem is taken place.

All kinds of initial bid values are available in NDSSA. We only focus on solving the second counterattack strategy, increasing bids slowly, by restricting bid increments. The essential bid increment is called as Minimum Increase Price (MIP) in this paper. Each advertiser is allowed to propose only the bid value which is either equal to that in the last round or increased by the MIP value. Thus, advertisers will bid actively due to MIP consideration.

For SEP, the first issue in NDSSA is the convergence speed. After NDSSA begins, each advertiser continuously updates his/her bid value to compete better slot. SEP's revenue is improved during this phase. When no advertiser would like to propose higher bid, NDSSA is converged. Requiring more rounds to reach stable allocation is caused from that bids are increased slowly. So, the convergence speed is an important factor to evaluate the mechanism for SEP.

The second issue is SEP's revenue, and this is most interested by SEP. Since SEP's revenue comes from advertisers' payments, maximizing bid values in each round implies SEP's revenue is improved.

To determine MIP settings, two MIP strategies are proposed: fixed and adaptive MIP strategies. The MIP setting is invariant in each round in fixed MIP strategy. The idea of additive-increase/multiplicative-decrease (AIMD) is applied in adaptive MIP strategy to calculate MIP setting in each round.

Convergence speed and SEP's revenue are discussed in this paper. We proof that fixed MIP strategy converges faster than AIMD in most instances. On the other hand, SEP will obtain more revenue than fixed MIP strategy according to our experiment results.

In the following context, NDSSA is defined in section 2 which includes the mechanism, bidding strategy, and MIP strategies. The convergence speed issue is analyzed in section 3. SEP's revenue comparisons between different MIP strategies are measured by experiments in section 4. The conclusion and future works are shown in section 5.

1.1   Related Work

Most popular payment calculations in SSA are GSP [1] and Vickrey-Clarke-Groves auction (VCG) [2]. Each winner pays bid value ranked in the next slot and the social welfare gap between the winner leaves and joins the auction in GSP and VCG respectively.

Incentive compatibility is the major advantage of VCG. Advertisers are ranked by their advertising valuations, because bidding on other prices is not beneficial for each advertiser. For SEP's revenue and computation cost, VCG is not practical in real word applications [4]. Moreover, VCG is the revenue lower bound of GSP for SEP in some instances [2]. To build a more realistic mechanism, SEP should consider GSP.

Winning the slot to improve the utility is the natural objective of each advertiser. After receiving a satisfied allocation, no advertiser wishes for any deviation, and the auction meets the equilibrium result [5]. Edelman et al. apply the stable idea to define locally envy-free equilibrium [1].

Since the allocation is steady under locally envy-free equilibrium, SEP's revenue is invariant and expectable. Moreover, VCG is the revenue lower bound for SEP when advertisers bid truthfully [2]. Because the steady allocation is the natural target and produces expectable revenue for each advertiser and SEP respectively, winning an envy-free slot is the bidding behavior discussed in NDSSA.

The multi-round assumption is close to the real world instance. Major property in this assumption is that participants will learn from previous result [5]. Cary et al. study the "balance bidding strategy" in the multi-round SSA [7]. Similar to our work, Cary et al. restrict the bid value, but not all instances meet the steady allocation. The outcome stability is important for SEP due to the revenue expectation, so the stability is considered in NDSSA.

Restricting minimum bid prices has the same effect with MIP. Even-Dar et al. modified Tâtonnement process to compute the minimum bid value [8]. When applying the idea of Even-Dar et al., SEP will gains more revenue than VCG. If the auction efficiency is guaranteed, the mechanism is more useful for SEP.

2   NDSSA

SEP must solve the revenue loss problem when applying GSP in multi-round SSA. Consider the advertiser occupied 1st slot, for example. If he/she is benefited in the 2nd slot, he/she will propose a lower bid price for moving to 2nd slot in the next round. The advertiser is benefited by payment decrease, but SEP revenue is reduced simultaneously.

2.1   Auction Mechanism

An NDSSA instance includes an SEP, and $k + 1$ advertisers that compete for k advertising slots. Suppose that each advertiser is interested in the same keyword and has the ability to update his/her bid value in each round. Payments are calculated by GSP, i.e. $p_i^x = b_{i+1}^x$, where p_i^x is ad_i's payment in x^{th} round and b_{i+1}^x is ad_{i+1}'s bid in x^{th} round.

Each advertiser ad_i has two parameters: the valuation and the initial bid rate (IBR) IBR_i. The valuation v_i is the worth per each click, and IBR indicates the ratio of valuation to the initial bid value. So the initial bid value is $v_i \times IBR_i$.

In x^{th} round, each advertiser is allowed to propose two kinds of bids b_i^x.

1. same bid value , i.e. $b_i^x = b_i^{x-1}$, or
2. higher value, i.e. $b_i^x \geq b_i^{x-1} + MIP^{x-1} + \epsilon, \forall \epsilon \geq 0$.

where all advertisers obey the same MIP value in each round.

Each slot sl_j has a click probability, called click-through rate (CTR), to simulate the slot importance. Without Lost of Generality, the better slot has higher CTR value. Therefore, ad_i allocated in sl_j pays $b_y^x \times CTR_j$ expectedly, where ad_y is the winner of sl_{j+1}.

2.2   Bidding Strategy

Consider ad_i occupies sl_j, the utility in x^{th} round is denoted by $u_i^x(j) = CTR_j \times (v_i - p_i^x)$. We only consider *Rational Bidding* advertiser in this paper. This implies no advertiser will bid higher than his/her valuation, i.e. $b_i^x \leq v_i$.

According to the concept of locally envy-free equilibrium, b_i^x will be increased only when sl_{j-1} is more beneficial than sl_j, i.e. $u_i^x(j-1) > u_i^x(j)$. Thus, ad_i will bid $\min\{(b_y^x + 1), (b_i^x + MIP)\}$, where ad_y is ranked in sl_{j-1}

2.3   MIP Strategies

The MIP value of fixed MIP strategy determines SEP's revenue. For higher settings, higher bid increment will limit the final bid value. Advertisers can not bid close to their valuations, so SEP's revenue in higher MIP setting may be less than in lower MIP setting. Consider the advertiser with valuation 50, bid value 40, and MIP 11, for example. The advertiser must propose $51 at least. According to rational bidding, SEP will lose $10 at most.

AIMD is used to probing unknown bandwidth in a TCP connection [3]. We apply the adjustability of AIMD to determine the MIP setting in each round. No bid update indicates the congestion in TCP, so the MIP value is set to one half. Otherwise, MIP is increased by one continuously. When each advertiser keeps the same bid under $MIP = 1$, advertisers have no idea to increase bids, and NDSSA converges.

To maximizing SEP's revenue, AIMD requires more rounds than fixed MIP strategy to check that NDSSA converges or not. SEP has the trade-off between the convergence speed and the revenue for determining MIP strategies.

3   Convergence Speed Analysis

3.1   Fixed MIP Strategy

SEP requires determining the MIP value before NDSSA begins. The MIP setting
is invariant throughout the auction. In the worst case, Theorem 1 shows the
number of rounds required to converge by fixed MIP strategy.

Theorem 1. *Consider ad_{mab} has maximum available bid amount over all advertisers in an NDSSA instance, where MIP^0 is initial MIP setting and $mab = \arg\max_{\forall i \neq 1} v_i(1 - IBR_i)$. In the worst case, the number of rounds r^F required to meet the stable allocation by fixed MIP strategy is as follows.*

$$r^F = \lceil \frac{v_{mab}(1 - IBR_{mab})}{MIP^0} \rceil$$

Proof. This proof is divided into two portions. We first deal with why the advertiser ad_{mab} dominates the convergence speed and then calculate the number of convergence rounds.

The advertiser ad_{mab}, where $mab = \arg\max_{\forall i \neq 1} v_i(1 - IBR_i)$, represents that he/she has most available prices to bid. In other words, ad_{mab} still can increase his/her bid value while others meet their valuations. The advertiser with highest valuation is excluded, because he/she will win the 1st slot when bidding over 2nd ranked advertiser rather than his/her valuation. Therefore, ad_{mab}, except for ad_1, dominates the convergence bottleneck in fixed MIP strategy.

We have the maximum available bid increment $v_{mab}(1 - IBR_{mab})$, and the increment divided by the MIP setting is the number of convergence rounds required in the worst case.

3.2   AIMD

The convergence speed of AIMD is analyzed by two portions. The first part is the first decrease of MIP value, and the second portion is the remainder rounds. They are shown in Lemma 1 and 2.

Lemma 1. *In the worst case of the NDSSA with AIMD, MIP^{h+1} will be decreased, where $h = \sqrt[2]{(MIP^0)^2 + 2v_{mab}} - MIP^0$.*

Proof. Suppose the MIP value is decreased at $(h + 1)^{th}$ round. All bids in h^{th} and $(h + 1)^{th}$ rounds are the same, i.e. $b_i^h = b_i^{h+1}$. In Fig. 1, the bid value is $b_{mab}^h + MIP^h$ where $MIP^h = MIP^0 + h$, and the pink area indicates the sum of bid increments in the auction, that is $h \times (MIP^0 + (MIP^0 + h))/2$.

If ad_{mab} still increases his/her bid in $(h + 1)^{th}$ round, he/she will overbid, i.e. $b_{mab}^h + MIP^h \geq v_{mab}$. The first round of MIP decrease h can be derived.

$$b_{mab}^h + MIP^h \geq v_{mab}$$
$$h \times (MIP^0 + (MIP^0 + h)) \geq 2v_{mab}$$
$$h^2 + 2MIP^0 h - 2v_{mab} \geq 0$$

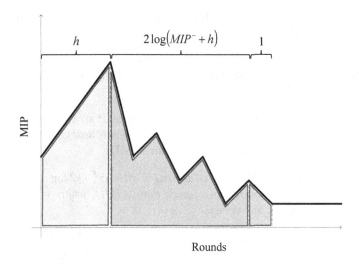

Fig. 1. The MIP modification history of NDSSA in the worst case

$$h \geq \frac{-2MIP^0 \pm \sqrt[2]{4(MIP^0)^2 + 8v_{mab}}}{2}$$
$$= \sqrt[2]{(MIP^0)^2 + 2v_{mab}} - MIP^0$$

According to Lemma 1, we derive that higher initial MIP settings result in faster convergence. Then, we focus on the remainder rounds in the worst case.

Lemma 2. *After first MIP decrease, NDSSA with AIMD requires* $2\lceil\log(MIP^0 + h)\rceil$ *rounds to converge, where* $h = \sqrt[2]{(MIP^0)^2 + 2v_{mab}} - MIP^0$ *and* $mab = \arg\max_{\forall i \neq 1} v_i(1 - IBR_i)$ *in the worst case.*

Proof. As shown in Fig. 1, the available bid increment is at most $MIP^0 + h$ in $(h+1)^{th}$ round. If the assumption is false, $MIP^0 + h + 1$ for example, ad_{mab} is able to update his/her bid in $(h+1)^{th}$ round due to $MIP^{h+1} = (MIP^0 + h) + 1$.

The remainder rounds in the worst case is composed of decrease-increase pairs. Consider the idea in $(h+2)^{th}$ round. We have $MIP^{h+2} = MIP^{h+1}/2 = (MIP^0 + h + 1)/2$ and the available bid increment is $MIP^0 + h$. So ad_{mab} increases his/her bid by $(MIP^0 + h + 1)/2$. The remainder bid increment is $(MIP^0+h)-(MIP^0+h+1)/2 = (MIP^0+h-1)/2$ in the first round of decrease-increase pair, and the MIP value should be increased by one. Because the MIP value is higher than the available bid increment, e.g. $((MIP^0 + h + 1)/2) + 1 \geq (MIP^0 + h - 1)/2$, no bid update will be taken place in the second round of decrease-increase pair.

The NDSSA with AIMD will decrease the MIP setting to one half, and each decrease contains a pair of rounds. When $MIP = 1$, each advertiser will no longer update his/her bid value. Therefore, the remainder rounds is $2\lceil\log(MIP^h)\rceil = 2\lceil\log(MIP^0 + h)\rceil$.

Combining Lemma 1 and 2, the total number of convergence rounds required by the NDSSA with AIMD is shown in Theorem 2.

Theorem 2. *NDSSA with AIMD will converge at most* $r^A = h + 2\lceil\log(MIP^0 + h)\rceil$ *rounds, where* $h = \sqrt[2]{(MIP^0)^2 + 2v_{mab}} - MIP^0$ *and* $mab = \arg\max_{\forall i \neq 1} v_i(1 - IBR_i)$.

The upper bound of convergence rounds for fixed MIP strategy and AIMD are shown in Theorem 1 and 2 respectively. Now, we are analyzing the condition that fixed MIP strategy converges faster than AIMD.

Theorem 3. *When the MIP value is decreased after* $(r^F - 2\log v_{mab})$ *rounds in AIMD, fixed MIP strategy converges faster than AIMD, where* $r^F = \lceil v_{mab}(1 - IBR_{mab})/MIP^0 \rceil$, *in the worst case.*

Proof. Combining Theorem 1 and 2, assume that fixed MIP strategy converges faster than AIMD, i.e. $r^F \leq r^A$. The objective is to proof $h \geq r^F - 2\log v_{mab}$.

$$
\begin{aligned}
r^F &\leq r^A \\
&= h + 2\log(MIP^0 + h) \\
&\leq h + 2\log(\frac{v_{mab}}{2}) + 2 \\
&= h + 2\log v_{mab} \\
\Rightarrow h &\geq r^F - 2\log v_{mab}
\end{aligned}
$$

4   Simulation

The distributions of valuation, CTR, and IBR, are shown in table 1, 2, and 3 respectively. The gaps of valuation and CTR settings include uniform, linear, exponential increasing, exponential decreasing, and random. The IBR settings are not required to restrict as a decreasing order, so the previous advertiser may have smaller IBR value than the next one. Since the maximum valuation is 50, initial MIP values are evaluated from 1 to 50 for each instance. So, we have 6250 measurements.

Following experiments are evaluated in this paper: (1) robustness, comparing which mechanism produces more SEP's revenue in more instances, (2) overall SEP's revenue comparison, evaluating SEP's revenue for all mechanisms under stable allocations, (3) SEP's average revenue, analyzing SEP's average revenue after converging, and (4) SEP's long-term revenue comparison, discussing the SEP's total revenue during a specific round.

4.1   Robustness

For two mechanisms x and y, we say that x is more robust than y if the number of instances with more SEP's revenue in x is more than that in y.

Table 1. Valuation settings

case #	ad_1	ad_2	ad_3	ad_4	ad_5
1	50	40	30	20	10
2	50	34	22	14	10
3	50	46	38	26	10
4	50	45	38	26	10
5	44.46	41.00	40.68	28.80	26.96

Table 2. CTR settings

case #	sl_1	sl_2	sl_3	sl_4
1	0.8	0.6	0.4	0.2
2	0.8	0.376	0.164	0.053
3	0.8	0.747	0.641	0.429
4	0.8	0.76	0.4	0.38
5	0.8	0.598	0.475	0.39

Table 3. IBR settings

case #	ad_1	ad_2	ad_3	ad_4	ad_5
1	0.9	0.7	0.5	0.3	0.1
2	0.1	0.3	0.5	0.7	0.9
3	0.9	0.3	0.7	0.1	0.5
4	0.5	0.1	0.7	0.3	0.9
5	0.87	0.36	0.57	0.10	0.92

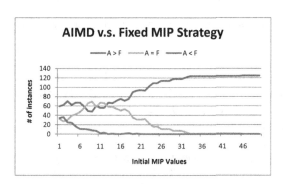

Fig. 2. SEP's revenue comparison between AIMD and fixed MIP strategy in the stable allocation.

The pairwise comparisons of fixed MIP strategy, AIMD, and VCG are evaluated in this experiment, and results are shown in Figure 2, 3, and 4. The labels $x > y$, $x = y$, and $x < y$ in each figure denote the number of instances that SEP's revenue of mechanism x is more than, same to, and less than mechanism y respectively.

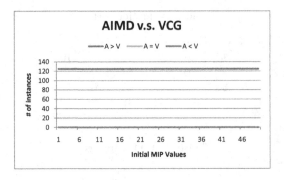

Fig. 3. SEP's revenue comparison between AIMD and VCG in the stable allocation

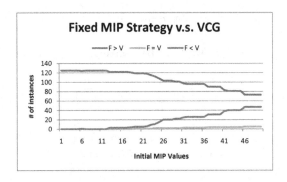

Fig. 4. SEP's revenue comparison between fixed MIP strategy and VCG in the stable allocation

In Figure 2, AIMD is more robust than fixed MIP strategy. After initial MIP 46, SEP gains more revenue in AIMD than in fixed MIP strategy in all instances. Recall our claim in suction 2.3: higher MIP values will increase the gap between stable bid value and the valuation for fixed MIP strategy. The conjecture is confirmed in this measurement.

The robustness comparison between AIMD and VCG is shown in Figure 3. AIMD is also more robust than VCG. SEP's revenue in VCG is the lower bound of that in GSP just in some instances [1]. The revenue lower bound of GSP is extended to all instances in NDSSA according to our simulation.

Figure 4 draws the comparison between fixed MIP strategy and VCG. As the initial MIP increases, fixed MIP strategy performs worse and worse. The disadvantage of fixed MIP strategy, less SEP's revenue in higher MIP settings, is explored clearly in this simulation. Under lower MIP settings, SEP is benefited, and fixed MIP strategy is more robust than VCG in average.

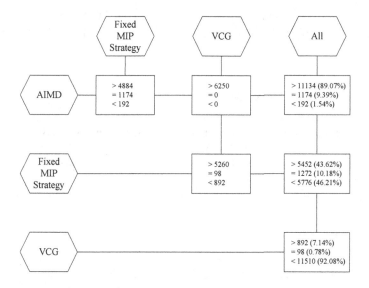

Fig. 5. Overall SEP's revenue comparison between all mechanisms

4.2   Overall SEP's Revenue Comparison

Fig 5 shows the overall comparison about SEP's revenue between AIMD, fixed MIP strategy, and VCG. Each square includes three comparison results: ">", "=", and "<", and they stand for how many instances that the left mechanism is better than, equal to, and worse than above one respectively. The VCG-ALL comparison, for example, represents that VCG produces more SEP's revenue than all mechanisms in 892 instances, identical to 98 instances, and less than in 11510 instances.

AIMD produces more revenue in 11134 instances (89.07%) approximately, and only 192 instances (1.54%) are worse than other mechanisms. The second one is the NDSSA with fixed MIP strategy, and last one is VCG. Comparing to

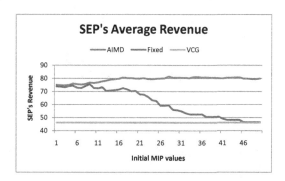

Fig. 6. SEP's average revenue comparison under different initial MIP values

VCG, AIMD improves 990 instances (15.84%) of fixed MIP strategy. Therefore, SEP's revenue of the stable allocation is maximized by adopting AIMD in most instances.

4.3   SEP's Average Revenue

In this simulation, we deal with the impact of initial MIP values on SEP's revenue in the stable allocation. Figure 6 shows the result. The x-axis indicates initial MIP values, and the y-axis is SEP's revenue averaged by all instances under the same MIP value.

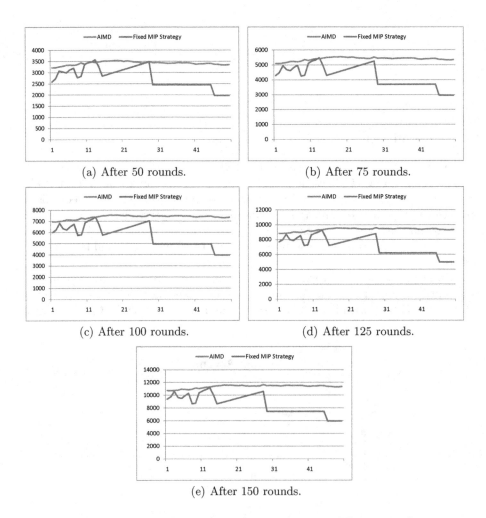

(a) After 50 rounds.   (b) After 75 rounds.

(c) After 100 rounds.   (d) After 125 rounds.

(e) After 150 rounds.

Fig. 7. SEP's total revenue comparison for given different rounds

Since the payment of VCG is calculated according to valuations, SEP's revenue is identical to various initial MIP values. In average, AIMD and fixed MIP strategy perform better than VCG.

AIMD receives a more stable result than fixed MIP strategy, and the impact of initial MIP values is slight. Since AIMD adjust MIP values in each round, bid values are optimized in average.

SEP's revenue of fixed MIP strategy decreases slightly in lower initial MIP settings. After initial MIP is 18 approximately, SEP's revenue drops dramatically until MIP 46. Increasing initial MIP value implies that the gap between the valuation and the stable bid value becomes larger. Therefore, SEP's revenue is decreased. Lower initial MIP values are better for SEP's revenue in the stable allocation.

4.4   SEP's Long-Term Revenue Comparison

Given a maximum round, the long-term revenue of SEP is the sum of revenue in each round. Only AIMD and fixed MIP strategy is compared in this simulation, and the result is shown in Figure 7.

Given different maximum rounds, the variance degree of SEP's long-term revenue is not different too much for both AIMD and fixed MIP strategy. Similar to Figure 6, initial MIP values almost do not vary SEP's total revenue in AIMD. SEP gains less revenue when initial MIP value increase in fixed MIP strategy. In Figure 7(a), SEP gains more revenue in fixed MIP strategy than AIMD in a few instances. As the number of maximum rounds increases, AIMD performs better in all initial MIP values. AIMD is more appropriate than fixed MIP strategy for the long term revenue for SEP.

5   Conclusion

When applying GSP to a multi-round SSA, SEP suffers the revenue loss problem. We propose Non-decreasing Sponsored Search Auction (NDSSA) to solve this problem while each advertiser is allowed to propose only non-decreasing bids in next round. Minimum Increase Price (MIP) is used in NDSSA to control the bid value for improving long term revenue.

Fixed MIP strategy and AIMD are applied to compute MIP values. For theoretical convergence speed analysis, fixed MIP strategy converges faster than AIMD in most instances. For SEP's revenue comparison of our simulations, AIMD not only produces better but is more robust than fixed MIP strategy. Thus, fixed MIP strategy is outstanding in short-term plan, and AIMD is for long-term consideration.

SEP's revenue is improved in NDSSA in this paper. However, SEP has no idea to capture advertiser's satisfaction. If the expected objectives, the utility for example, are not achieved, advertisers may leave the auction. SEP's revenue will also be decreased potentially. Therefore, measuring satisfactions for any participant will be studied in the future.

Acknowledgement. This work was supported in part by Taiwan NSC under grant no. NSC 98-2221-E-274-006 and NSC 99-2221-E-274-007. The author like to thank reviewers for their insightful comments which helped to significantly improve the paper.

References

1. Edelman, B., Ostrovsky, M., Schwarz, M.: Internet Advertising and the Generalized Second Price Auction: Selling Billions of Dollars Worth of Keywords. American Economic Review 97(1), 242–259 (2007)
2. Varian, H.R.: Position Auction. International Journal of Industrial Organization 25(6), 1163–1178 (2007)
3. Chiu, D.-M., Jain, R.: Analysis of the Increase and Decrease Algorithms for Congestion Avoidance in Computer Networks. Computer Networks and ISDN Systems 17(1), 1–14 (1989)
4. Rothkopf, M.H.: Thirteen Reasons Why the Vickrey-Clarke-Groves Process Is Not Practical. Operations Research 55(2), 191–197 (2007)
5. Nisan, N., Roughgarden, T., Tardos, E., Vazirani, V.V.: Algorithmic Game Theory. Cambridge University Press (2007)
6. Bu, T.M., Deng, X., Qi, Q.: Forward looking Nash equilibrium for keyword auction. Information Processing Letters 105, 41–46 (2008)
7. Cary, M., Das, A., Edelman, B., Giotis, I., Heimerl, K., Karlin, A.R., Mathieu, C., Schwarz, M.: Greedy Bidding Strategies for Keyword Auctions. In: Proceedings of the 8th ACM Conference on Electronic Commerce, pp. 262–271. ACM Press, San Diego (2007)
8. Even-Dar, E., Feldman, J., Mansour, Y., Muthukrishnan, S.M.: Position Auctions with Bidder-Specific Minimum Prices. In: Papadimitriou, C., Zhang, S. (eds.) WINE 2008. LNCS, vol. 5385, pp. 577–584. Springer, Heidelberg (2008)
9. Aggarwal, G., Goel, A., Motwani, R.: Truthful Auctions for Pricing Search Keywords. In: Proceedings of the 7th ACM Conference on Electronic Commerce, pp. 1–7. ACM Press, Ann Arbor (2006)

Acceptance Strategies for Maximizing Agent Profits in Online Scheduling

Mengxiao Wu[1], Mathijs de Weerdt[2], and Han La Poutré[1]

[1] Center for Mathematics and Computer Science (CWI), The Netherlands
[2] Delft University of Technology, The Netherlands
{wu,hlp}@cwi.nl, m.m.deweerdt@tudelft.nl

Abstract. In the global logistics market, agents need to decide upon whether to accept jobs offered sequentially. For each offer, an agent makes an immediate selection decision with little knowledge about future jobs; the goal is to maximize the profit. We study this online decision problem of acceptance of unit length jobs with time constraints, which involves online scheduling. We present theoretically optimal acceptance strategies for a fundamental case, and develop heuristic strategies in combination with an evolutionary algorithm for more general and complex cases. We show experimentally that in the fundamental case the performance of heuristic solutions is almost the same as that of theoretical solutions. In various settings, we compare the results achieved by our online solutions to those generated by the optimal offline solutions; the average-case performance ratios are about 1.1. We also analyze the impact of the ratio between the number of slots and the number of jobs on the difficulty of decisions and the performance of our solutions.

Keywords: Online decisions, Resource allocation, Admission control.

1 Introduction

Consider a market of global logistics in which a large number of jobs are dispatched day and night to many logistics companies. During a period of time, each company gets sequential offers of jobs from the market. Given its limited capacity and time resources, usually, a company can only accept part of the offers. Because of the competition in the market, we suppose the selection decisions are *immediate* and *irrevocable*. The company's target is to maximize its profit through selecting (and executing) jobs. This is an online decision problem, as the company makes the decision on each job offer without prior knowledge of future jobs. To solve it, we make an agent-based model for simulating the decision process of the company (an agent) in the market and design *acceptance strategies* (algorithms) for the agent's optimal decisions.

We first introduce our problem briefly. When job offers arrive one at a time, each job is characterized by a time window for scheduling and a payment. The agent needs to make a take-it-or-leave-it decision immediately. The agent must schedule and execute every accepted job within its time window so as to get its payment. The utility (profit) that the agent would get is the sum of the payments of all accepted jobs. In

E. David et al. (Eds.): AMEC/TADA 2011, LNBIP 119, pp. 115–128, 2013.

our analysis, we assume all jobs have the same processing time, i.e. one time slot, and the agent can execute only one job in each time slot. In this work, we focus on the selection decisions, so we make the scheduling part relatively easy, in which all jobs are assumed to be future activities and no execution happens during the whole offering process.

Our problem may be categorized as a variant of online admission control for interval scheduling [1,2,3]. In such problems, the interval between a job's release time and deadline equals the time window in our problem. The authors emphasize the immediate notification of whether to schedule each job at its arrival, which is similar to our selection decision. The decisions in our problem, however, are made at the jobs' offering time, which is not their release time, i.e. the earliest available time for execution. Hence, an accepted job can be rescheduled (within its time window) during the whole offering process. This point distinguishes our problem from almost all online interval scheduling/selection problems in previous work, in which decisions are made at the jobs' release time. Because no job will be executed during the decisions of the jobs that followed, the scheduling part of our problem is more flexible, which increases the complexity of selection. The reason is that with such flexibility in scheduling, the agent has higher expectations of future jobs, but these can also cause him to reject current jobs with good payments that he would otherwise accept.

The agent makes the decision on each job offer in two steps, i) whether this job can be feasibly scheduled together with all previously accepted jobs, and ii) when one or more feasible schedules exist, whether this job is worthy of taking. The focus of this work is on the acceptance strategies rather than the scheduling algorithms. We analyze theoretical solutions in a fundamental case and develop heuristic solutions in general and complex cases. We also present a general idea of using a theoretical analysis of a simple case to determine which are the most important parameters, and then using an evolutionary algorithm to find the optimal values of the parameters also in more complex settings. The approach presented in this work can be used to support online decisions in e-commerce applications related to logistics.

Typically, an online solution is evaluated by comparison with an optimal offline solution that knows the entire sequence of jobs in advance. In our experimental analysis, we use an *average-case performance ratio*, which is defined as the ratio between the average result generated by the optimal offline solution and the average result achieved by the online solution on a large number of instances. Our (theoretical and heuristic) solutions generate performance ratios around 1.1 in experiments with various settings. In the fundamental case, the performance of the heuristics is very close to that of the theoretically optimal online solutions. We also analyze the impact of the ratio between the number of slots and the number of jobs. The decision is most difficult when there are two to three times as many jobs as time slots.

The rest of this paper is organized as follows. We first present the problem model in Section 2 and then propose the solutions and acceptance strategies in Section 3. Following the descriptions, in Section 4, the performance of the strategies is evaluated and compared through experiments. Next, we give a brief summary of related work. Finally, conclusion and future work are given.

2 Problem Model

Suppose an agent is offered a finite set N of $n \in \mathbb{N}$ *independent* jobs sequentially. Each job $j \in N$ is characterized by a time window $[x_j, y_j]$ $(x_j, y_j \in \mathbb{N})$ and a payment $z_j \in [0, 1]$, which are independent of each other. Notice that the approach proposed by us works for any given range of payments, but we use the normalized values for ease of presentation. Every job's processing time is one time slot; it must be executed within the given time window. The agent has a set T of $t \in \mathbb{N}$ time slots available for all jobs in N. We let L denote the maximum length of all time windows where $1 \leq L \leq t$, so all jobs' time windows are in T. Given any subset of jobs $A \subseteq N$, we let $\mathcal{S}(A, T) = 1$ denote the existence of one (or more) feasible schedule such that every job $j \in A$ can be uniquely paired with a slot $i \in T$ where $x_j \leq i \leq y_j$. When a new job j is offered, the agent needs to judge whether the set of jobs $A_j \cup \{j\}$ can be feasibly scheduled first, where A_j denotes the set of jobs previously accepted before job j and $\mathcal{S}(A_j, T) = 1$. If $\mathcal{S}(A_j \cup \{j\}, T) = 1$, then the agent needs to make a decision to accept it or not, otherwise the agent can only reject it. Given the set of all accepted jobs $A \subseteq N$ (with $\mathcal{S}(A, T) = 1$), the utility U that the agent would get equals the sum of the payments of all accepted jobs, i.e. $U = \sum_{j \in A} z_j$.

3 Acceptance Strategies

A solution to the problem above is composed of two parts: a scheduling algorithm and an acceptance strategy. For each new job $j \in N$, we consider the scheduling problem of $A_j \cup \{j\}$ as a variant of the Bipartite Matching Problem. All slots T are on one side and all jobs in $A_j \cup \{j\}$ are on the other side; each job only connects to the slots of its time window. A feasible schedule is an one-sided matching in which every job is matched with one slot connected to it. We use the Ford-Fulkerson algorithm [4] to find this kind of matching between jobs in $A_j \cup \{j\}$ and slots in T. If $\mathcal{S}(A_j \cup \{j\}) = 1$, the agent then decides whether to take job j by using acceptance strategies.

  We first present two theoretical strategies for a fundamental case in which all jobs have unit time windows; we analyze how to calculate the optimal values of strategy parameters, which maximize the agent's expected utility. Next, we study a general case in which the maximum length of time windows is larger than one: it is very difficult to give analytic solutions for such a setting. Therefore, we develop heuristic strategies for the general case. At last, we give extensions of our strategies for a more complex case in which the precise number of jobs is unknown.

  Notice that in the rest of this paper, when we discuss the acceptance decision on a new job j, this is always based on the premise that job j can be feasibly scheduled together with previously accepted jobs in A_j.

3.1 Theoretical Strategies for Unit Time Windows

In this section, we study a fundamental case of the problem, in which every job j's time window is a single slot denoted by x_j. For theoretical analysis, we assume that the positions of all unit time windows are uniformly distributed on all slots T. We also assume that all jobs' payments are uniformly distributed on the range of $[0, 1]$.

Single Threshold. Perhaps the simplest acceptance strategy is setting a single threshold for the payments. If the new job j's payment is no less than a threshold $\alpha \in [0, 1]$, the agent will accept it. We let $\mathcal{D}_j = 1$ and $\mathcal{D}_j = 0$ denote the agent's acceptance and rejection of job j respectively. The single threshold strategy is given by

$$\mathcal{D}(j) = \begin{cases} 1 & \text{if } z_j \geq \alpha \text{ and } \mathcal{S}(A_j \cup \{j\}) = 1 \\ 0 & \text{otherwise} \end{cases} \tag{1}$$

We call this the *Theoretical Single Threshold strategy (T1T)*. Next, we present how to determine the theoretically optimal value of α, given the uniform distributions.

We let E^i denote the initially expected utility that the agent would get on each slot $i \in T$; the expected utility on all t slots is $E = t \cdot E^i$. Because t is a constant, the optimal value of α maximizing E^i also maximizes E. As we know, only if at least one job j with $(x_j = i) \wedge (z_j \geq \alpha)$ exists, slot i will finally be occupied by a job; the expected payment of the slot (and the job) is $(1 + \alpha)/2$. The probability of the existence of such job j equals 1 minus the probability that no job has a time window including slot i and a payment of at least α. Reasoning in this way, E^i is given by

$$\begin{aligned} E^i &= P\left(\exists\, j,\; x_j = i \wedge z_j \geq \alpha\right) \cdot \left(\frac{1+\alpha}{2}\right) \\ &= \{1 - [P\left(j \in N,\; x_j \neq i \vee z_j < \alpha\right)]^n\} \cdot \left(\frac{1+\alpha}{2}\right) \\ &= \left[1 - \left(1 - \frac{1-\alpha}{t}\right)^n\right] \cdot \left(\frac{1+\alpha}{2}\right) \end{aligned} \tag{2}$$

We can get the optimal value of α by solving formula $\frac{dE^i}{d\alpha} = \frac{1}{2} - \frac{1}{2}\left(1 - \frac{1-\alpha}{t}\right)^n - \frac{n}{2t}(1 + \alpha)\left(1 - \frac{1-\alpha}{t}\right)^{n-1} = 0$. In our experiments presented later, we solve it in an approximate way by searching α in $[0, 1]$ with step size of 0.001.

n Thresholds. During the whole offering process, the agents may need to make a total of (at most) n decisions: one for each job. In this section, we present a strategy with n thresholds instead of a single threshold for all jobs. If the new job j's payment is no less than the jth threshold $\alpha_j \in [0, 1]$, the agent will accept it. The strategy is given by

$$\mathcal{D}(j) = \begin{cases} 1 & \text{if } z_j \geq \alpha_j \text{ and } \mathcal{S}(A_j \cup \{j\}) = 1 \\ 0 & \text{otherwise} \end{cases} \tag{3}$$

We call this the *Theoretical n Thresholds strategy (TnT)*. Notice that the jth threshold α_j is independent of the jth job exactly offered.

We let E_j^i denote the expected utility that the agent would get on an available slot i when the jth job is offered. There are three possibilities. If job j's slot is slot i and its payment is no less than α_j, which happens with probability $1/t \cdot (1 - \alpha_j)$, the agent will accept it and get an expected payment $(1 + \alpha_j)/2$. Otherwise, if job j's payment is less than α_j (happening with probability $1/t \cdot \alpha_j$) or its slot is not slot i (happening with probability $(t - 1)/t$), the agent will reject it in the expectation of slot i for the next job $j + 1$. Therefore, the expected utility E_j^i is given by

Table 1. Simple example

(x_j, z_j)	$(2, 0.12)$	$(1, 0.83)$	$(3, 0.29)$	$(3, 0.41)$	$(2, 0.23)$	
$T1T$	N(< 0.295)	Y(> 0.295)	N(< 0.295)	Y(> 0.295)	N(< 0.295)	$U = 1.24$
TnT	N(< 0.435)	Y(> 0.368)	Y(> 0.282)	N($occupied$)	Y(> 0)	$U = 1.35$
Offline	N	Y	N	Y	Y	$U = 1.47$

$$E_j^i = \frac{1}{t} \cdot (1 - \alpha_j) \cdot \frac{1 + \alpha_j}{2} + \frac{1}{t} \cdot \alpha_j \cdot E_{j+1}^i + \frac{t-1}{t} \cdot E_{j+1}^i \tag{4}$$

We calculate the optimal value of α_j by solving formula $\frac{dE_j^i}{d\alpha_j} = \frac{E_{j+1}^i - \alpha_j}{t} = 0$ and get $\alpha_j = E_{j+1}^i$. So if job j's payment is no less than the agent's expectation of job $j + 1$, given any available slot, the agent will accept it. Otherwise, the agent should leave the slot to job $j + 1$ to get a possibly higher payment. As the expectation of job $n + 1$ is zero, $\alpha_n = 0$. Replacing E_j^i and E_{j+1}^i with α_{j-1} and α_j in Eq. (4) respectively, we get a recursive function $f(j, n, t)$ to calculate threshold α_j where $1 \leq j \leq n$.

$$\alpha_j = f(j, n, t) = \begin{cases} \frac{1}{2t} \cdot (f(j+1, n, t))^2 + \frac{t-1}{t} \cdot f(j+1, n, t) + \frac{1}{2t} & j < n \\ 0 & j \geq n \end{cases} \tag{5}$$

Given a fixed t and a sequence of n, we find that i) for each setting of t and n, threshold α_j is non-linear decreasing; ii) the smaller the n is, the faster the decreasing is; iii) the smaller the n is, the lower the first threshold α_1 is. These match with the intuition that given the same number of slots, the expectations and thus the thresholds decline faster when there are less (future) jobs.

Simple Example. Given their definitions, strategy $T1T$ is theoretically optimal (in expectation) among single-threshold strategies and strategy TnT is theoretically optimal (in expectation) among n-threshold strategies in the fundamental case. We use a simple example with five jobs and three slots to illustrate the differences. In Table 1, the pairs of (x_j, z_j) in the first row represent the jobs in order of arrival (from left to right) where $1 \leq j \leq 5$. In the subsequent rows, the decisions are followed by the thresholds for both of the strategies. Although TnT loses some utility on the fourth job by accepting the third one, the advantage of the adaptive thresholds of TnT shows in accepting the last job in spite of its relatively low payment.

3.2 Heuristic Strategies

In the fundamental case above, once a job is accepted, its schedule is fixed. However, the length of time windows is generally not unit. The flexibility of (re)scheduling benefits applicability while increasing the difficulty of decisions. In this general case, even if all distributions are sill uniform, it is hard to get the optimal values of thresholds in the above way, given the multiple possibilities of time windows and tremendous possibilities of (re)scheduling. Hence, it is necessary to consider approximate solutions. In this section, we therefore develop heuristic strategies. The basic idea is using multiple parameters to define a decision function; their optimal values are learned by an evolutionary algorithm (EA) [5] through a large number of training sessions.

Single Threshold. The first heuristic strategy proposed by us is similar to the theoretical single threshold strategy defined by Eq. (1) except that the optimal value of $\alpha \in [0, 1]$ is determined by the EA. We call this the *Heuristic Single Threshold strategy* ($H1T$); its performance is expected to be very close to that of $T1T$ in the fundamental case.

n Thresholds. Analogously, we also try a heuristic strategy of a different threshold for each job similar to the theoretical one defined by Eq. (3), but let the EA search the optimal combination of the values of those n thresholds $\alpha_j \in [0, 1]$ where $1 \leq j \leq n$. We call this the *Heuristic n Thresholds strategy* (HnT).

Three Thresholds. This strategy divides the whole offering process into three stages by using two parameters $\beta_1, \beta_2 \in [0, 1]$ ($\beta_1 < \beta_2$) and sets a single threshold $\alpha_k \in [0, 1]$ ($1 \leq k \leq 3$) for jobs' payments per stage. The agent will accept job j which is offered in the kth stage only if its payment is no less than α_k. The whole strategy is given by

$$\mathcal{D}(j) = \begin{cases} 1 & \text{if } j \leq \beta_1 \cdot n, \ z_j \geq \alpha_1, \text{ and } \mathcal{S}(A_j \cup \{j\}) = 1 \\ 1 & \text{if } \beta_1 \cdot n < j \leq \beta_2 \cdot n, \ z_j \geq \alpha_2, \text{ and } \mathcal{S}(A_j \cup \{j\}) = 1 \\ 1 & \text{if } j > \beta_2 \cdot n, \ z_j \geq \alpha_3, \text{ and } \mathcal{S}(A_j \cup \{j\}) = 1 \\ 0 & \text{otherwise} \end{cases} \tag{6}$$

We call this the *Heuristic 3 Thresholds strategy* ($H3T$).

Linear Function. To be more precise than the strategies with one or three thresholds for payments, we propose heuristic strategies based on *Piecewise Linear Functions* (PLF). As they have fewer parameters to be learned by the EA, it will be easier and faster to find the optimal solutions than the n threshold strategies. The simplest one is a linear function ($PLF1$). We set one parameter α as the slope of the linear function which generates the thresholds for payments, and also set a parameter γ to determine the constant. The agent will accept job j, if its payment is no less than the threshold given by function $p(j)$. The whole strategy is defined by

$$\mathcal{D}(j) = \begin{cases} 1 & \text{if } z_j \geq p(j) \text{ and } \mathcal{S}(A_j \cup \{j\}) = 1 \\ 0 & \text{otherwise} \end{cases}$$

$$\text{where } p(j) = \alpha \cdot j + \gamma \tag{7}$$

To find the global optimum of parameters α and γ for the PLF-based heuristics, we use the EA to learn these within a reasonable range. Any threshold is only reasonable within the range of $[0, 1]$, so $\gamma \in [0, 1]$. Next, given that $j \in \mathbb{N}$ and $z_j \in [0, 1]$, we can derive the range for α as follows.

$$0 \leq \alpha \cdot j + \gamma \leq 1 \text{ and } \gamma \in [0, 1] \Longrightarrow \alpha \cdot j \in [-1, 1] \Longrightarrow \alpha \in [-1, 1].$$

Two-Piece Piecewise Linear Function. The second PLF-based strategy is a two-piece piecewise linear function ($PLF2$). One parameter $\beta \in [0,1]$ cuts the whole offering process into two stages. The slopes of these two pieces are $\alpha_1, \alpha_2 \in [-1,1]$ and the constant of the first piece is $\gamma \in [0,1]$. The agent will accept job j, if its payment is no less than the threshold given by function $p(j)$. The strategy is defined by

$$\mathcal{D}(j) = \begin{cases} 1 & \text{if } z_j \geq p(j) \text{ and } \mathcal{S}(A_j \cup \{j\}) = 1 \\ 0 & \text{otherwise} \end{cases}$$

$$\text{where} \quad p(j) = \begin{cases} \alpha_1 \cdot j + \gamma & \text{if } j \leq \beta \cdot n \\ \alpha_2 \cdot j + (\alpha_1 - \alpha_2) \cdot \beta \cdot n + \gamma & \text{if } j > \beta \cdot n \end{cases} \tag{8}$$

Three-Piece Piecewise Linear Function. The last one is a three-piece piecewise linear function ($PLF3$). The whole process is divided into three stages by two parameters $\beta_1, \beta_2 \in [0,1]$ where $\beta_1 < \beta_2$. The slopes of the three pieces are $\alpha_1, \alpha_2, \alpha_3 \in [-1,1]$. The constant of the first piece is $\gamma \in [0,1]$. Similarly, the thresholds are still given by function $p(j)$ and the strategy is defined by

$$\mathcal{D}(j) = \begin{cases} 1 & \text{if } z_j \geq p(j) \text{ and } \mathcal{S}(A_j \cup \{j\}) = 1 \\ 0 & \text{otherwise} \end{cases}$$

$$\text{where} \quad p(j) = \begin{cases} \alpha_1 \cdot j + \gamma & \text{if } j \leq \beta_1 \cdot n \\ \alpha_2 \cdot j + (\alpha_1 - \alpha_2) \cdot \beta_1 \cdot n + \gamma & \text{if } \beta_1 \cdot n < j \leq \beta_2 \cdot n \\ \begin{aligned} &\alpha_3 \cdot j + (\alpha_1 - \alpha_2) \cdot \beta_1 \cdot n \\ &+ (\alpha_2 - \alpha_3) \cdot \beta_2 \cdot n + \gamma \end{aligned} & \text{if } j > \beta_2 \cdot n \end{cases} \tag{9}$$

3.3 Dealing with Uncertainty over the Number of Jobs

For the strategies presented above, the number of jobs n is required as an input. We extend the model to a more general case where the total number of jobs is unknown until the whole offering process finishes. Instead of the precise number of jobs n, the agent is only given a range of $[n_{min}, n_{max}]$ and a random distribution. In this work, we assume that n is always uniformly distributed on the range.

For the theoretical strategy $T1T$, it is straightforward to use the expected value of n to calculate the optimal value of the single threshold. This variant of $T1T$ is still theoretically optimal. However, we cannot immediately use the expected value of n in the theoretical strategy TnT, because the expected value changes after job $j > n_{min}$.

We propose an approximate solution based on TnT. We let $\bar{n}$ denote the initially expected value of n, i.e. $\bar{n} = (n_{min} + n_{max})/2$, which is consistent with the offering process until job n_{min} is offered. The agent can calculate threshold α_j by Eq. (5) with input $\bar{n}$ until $j = n_{min}$. After that $j > n_{min}$, the agent's expectation of n is changed by each new offer. We treat the distributions on the range of $[j, n_{max}]$ approximately as uniform distributions. We let $\hat{n}$ denote the average of j and n_{max}, i.e. $\hat{n} = (j + n_{max})/2$. For jobs still coming after job n_{min}, the agent calculates α_j based on $\hat{n}$ instead of $\bar{n}$. The formal definition is given by

$$\mathcal{D}(j) = \begin{cases} 1 & \text{if } z_j \geq \alpha_j \text{ and } \mathcal{S}(A_j \cup \{j\}) = 1 \\ 0 & \text{otherwise} \end{cases}$$

where

$$\alpha_j = \begin{cases} f(j, \bar{n}, t) & \text{if } j \le n_{min} \\ f(j, \hat{n}, t) & \text{if } n_{min} < j \le n_{max} \end{cases}$$

$$\bar{n} = \lfloor \frac{n_{min} + n_{max}}{2} \rfloor, \ \hat{n} = \lfloor \frac{j + n_{max}}{2} \rfloor \tag{10}$$

where $f(j, n, t)$ is defined in Eq. (5).

To ensure that the heuristics define a threshold for any possible time slot, we replace n by n_{max} in their definitions. By using a representative training set for the EA, the found parameters then incorporate the distribution of n over the range of $[n_{min}, n_{max}]$.

4   Experiments

In the previous sections, we presented two theoretical strategies: $T1T$, TnT and six heuristic strategies: $H1T$, HnT, $H3T$, $PLF1$, $PLF2$ and $PLF3$. In order to evaluate and compare their performance, we set up various experiments. The experimental setting includes the number of jobs n, the number of slots t, the maximum length of time windows L, the random distribution of the starts of time windows x_j, the random distribution of the length of time windows, and the random distribution of payments z_j where $j \in N$. The length of all jobs' time windows is uniformly distributed on the range of $[1, L]$, unless the randomly generated start of the time window plus the maximum length exceeds the slots, i.e. $x_j + L - 1 > t$. In this case, the range is reduced to $[1, t - x_j + 1]$ and the length is uniformly distributed on this new range. The variable settings will be specified when we present the experiments one by one below.

Typically, the performance of online solutions is evaluated by the comparison with the problem's optimal offline solutions. The offline version of our problem is a variant of the Rectangular Assignment Problem, which can be solved by the Hungarian Algorithm [6]. In this work, we use an implementation in MATLAB [7].

Figure 1 illustrates the experimental flow that we follow for each experiment in this work. For instance, given an experimental setting, a theoretical strategy and a heuristic strategy, the experiment will be performed in two stages. First, for the heuristic strategy, use the EA to search the optimal combination of the values of its parameters, given 100 sets of n jobs. Each evaluation of the EA includes 100 simulations based on the 100 instances and the evaluation fitness is defined by the average of the 100 simulation outcomes. As the result, we get an optimal combination of the parameters' values. The heuristic strategy and the optimal values of its parameters form a heuristic solution. Repeat this part 10 times with different sets of 100 instances; 10 heuristic solutions are achieved. Second, cross-evaluate the 10 heuristic solutions by simulations with new 2000 sets of n jobs. The theoretical strategy is also evaluated on the same 2000 instances. To generate benchmarks, we also let the optimal offline solution work on the same 2000 instances in this step.

In this way, for each setting, we get 2000 results of each theoretical strategy and 10×2000 results of every heuristic strategy. We define the performance of a theoretical strategy by the average of the 2000 results. For a heuristic, the average of the 2000

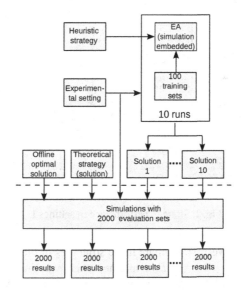

Fig. 1. Experimental flow

Table 2. Experimental settings I

t	n	t/n	L
30	$90, 75, 50, 35$	$0.33, 0.4, 0.6, 0.86$	1
$15, 50, 70$	75	$0.2, 0.67, 0.93$	1

results of each solution indicates the solution's performance. We then define the performance of a heuristic strategy by the average of the 10 averages of different solutions. We also have 2000 results of the optimal offline solution. We define the ratio between the average of the 2000 results achieved by the optimal offline solution and the performance of an online strategy to be the average-case performance ratio, which is no less than 1. The smaller the performance ratio is, the better the online solution performs.

A guideline for the EA's population size is given as at least $17 + 3 \cdot m^{1.5}$ where m is the number of parameters [5]. The number of parameters of HnT is the same as the number of jobs; the maximum n that we plan to experiment is 110. The numbers of parameters of all the other heuristics are constants: the maximum one is 6. Therefore, we set the population size as 3000 for HnT and set it as 1000 for other heuristics, which are quite sufficient. We also set the EA's evaluation limit as one million. These settings guarantee that the convergence happens before the evaluation limit is reached, so the (near) optimal results can be found.

4.1   Known Number of Jobs

First, we evaluate all strategies in two cases, unit time windows ($L = 1$) and general time windows ($L \geq 1$), under the environment that the number of jobs n is known. Both cases use the same 7 settings (Table 2); all distributions are uniform distributions.

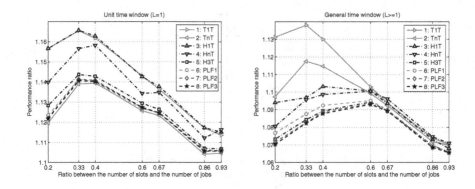

Fig. 2. Strategy performance in settings I

Unit Time Windows. We first compare these strategies in the case of unit time windows, in which strategies $T1T$ and TnT are theoretically optimal. Besides them, the n thresholds strategy is regarded as a more precise one. Therefore, we expect that strategies TnT and HnT will perform best in this case.

Figure 2 (left) illustrates the experimental results. As we expected, the performance of TnT is best in all settings. All PLF-based strategies perform very close to the benchmarks of the online solutions set by TnT; the three-piece one, i.e. $PLF3$, is the best among them. As the three thresholds of $H3T$ are constants, its performance is slightly worse than that of the PLF-based strategies. Because of the n thresholds, the performance of HnT was expected to be close to that of TnT, but it actually performs worse than the PLF-based strategies and $H3T$ here. One reason is that the size of training sets, i.e. 100 instances per evaluation, is sufficient for other heuristics but is not big enough to prevent over-fitting of the n parameters of HnT. Hence, the results are not optimal in general. By increasing the size of training sets for HnT, the problem can be resolved but the searching time will be significantly extended. The two single threshold strategies perform worst but the largest performance ratio is still small. When the single parameter of heuristic $H1T$ is learned by the EA sufficiently, its performance is almost the same as that of the theoretical strategy $T1T$.

In Figure 2 (left), we notice that the worst performance of all strategies is generated at the point of $t/n = 0.33$; the performance at its right point $t/n = 0.4$ is also low. On one side, when ratio t/n is very close to 1, as the distribution of positions is uniform, each slot is expected to assign one job. The agent's decisions are relatively easy without considering future jobs too much. On the other side, when ratio t/n is very close to 0, each slot is expected to assign many jobs. Because of the uniform distribution of payments, the decisions are also relatively easy: the agent only accepts jobs with very high payments. When the decision problem is easier, the performance of all strategies will be better. The middle area is the most difficult part, in which the agent is indeed in a dilemma between the current job and the expectation/uncertainty of future jobs. Even in this part, however, TnT and $PLF3$ can still generate performance ratios around 1.14.

Table 3. Experimental settings II

t	n	$t/\bar{n}$	L
30	$[70, 110], [70, 80], [35, 65], [30, 40]$	$0.33, 0.4, 0.6, 0.86$	5
$15, 50, 60$	$[60, 90]$	$0.2, 0.67, 0.8$	5

General Time Windows. We extend to the case of general time windows. This increases the flexibility of scheduling and also the difficulty of decisions. As our theoretical strategies are derived from the case of unit time windows, their threshold values are no longer optimal in this general case. We still evaluate them here to show the change.

Figure 2 (right) illustrates the experimental results. We notice that when ratio $t/n \geq 0.6$, the performance ratios of all strategies are very close. The reason is, as we mentioned, the decision problem becomes easier in this part as the agent knows that there is a little choice on every slot. On the side of $t/n < 0.6$, the performance of strategies is clearly distinguished. Compared to $T1T$, we find that $H1T$ performs much better, although both of them use a single threshold. This indicates the advantage of the heuristic. By using the EA, the strategy can learn to find the good solutions in various settings. Compared to the results of unit time windows shown in Figure 2 (left), we find that the performance ratios are decreased (so the results are better). We will study the impact of the length of time windows on the performance of the heuristics in our future work. As we expected, the theoretical strategies (derived from the case of unit time windows) perform significantly worse than other heuristics here, because they cannot adapt to the change of the length of time windows.

4.2 Unknown Number of Jobs

The previous experiments evaluated the strategies where the number of jobs n is known. Next, we study the performance of our solutions where n is unknown but uniformly distributed over a given range . Table 3 shows a new set of 7 settings. The expectations of n in all settings correspond to the values of n in Table 2. Although strategy HnT provides good solutions in previous experiments, we omit it in the following experiments with consideration of the cost of experimental time.

Unit Time Windows. We compare the strategies under settings with unit time windows and unknown n. As we described, when we use the expectation of n instead of n for $T1T$, the resulting α is still theoretically optimal. Although the approximate variant of TnT is no longer strictly optimal in the theoretical analysis, we think the difference between the approximate solution and the theoretical solution is very small.

Figure 3 (left) illustrates the experimental results. Apparently, TnT still performs best as we expected. The value of the threshold of $T1T$ is still theoretically optimal and the performance of $H1T$ is very close to that of $T1T$. Totally, the performance ratios of all strategies in this case are very similar to those generated in the same settings (except for the issue of n) shown in Figure 2 (left). Considering the increased complexity of the problem, our solutions are robust under dynamic environments.

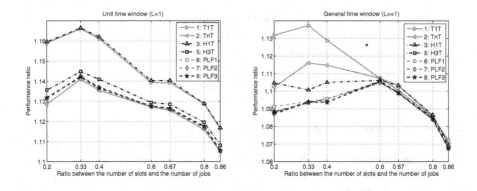

Fig. 3. Strategy performance in settings II

General Time Windows. Analogously, we also evaluate the strategies in the case of general time windows and unknown n. Figure 3 (right) illustrates the experimental results, which are quite similar to those shown in Figure 2 (right), except for the results where $t/n = 0.2$. This indicates the robust and adaptive properties of our approach of defining key parameters and using the EA to learn their optimal values.

4.3 Non-uniform Distributions

Further, we evaluate the strategies in more general and complex settings where the random distributions of the starts of time windows and the payments are non-uniform distributions. We experiment various settings, e.g. all payments being exponentially distributed or all starts being normally distributed around a slot close to one end of T; the resulting average-case performance ratios are between 1.09 to 1.22.

5 Related Work

Our problem relates to the online weighted bipartite matching problem, which is to assign each of sequentially arriving requests to one of the servers given in advance to maximize/minimize the total weight of the matching being produced [8,9]. Instead of accepting all requests, we focus on selecting a subset of requests to maximize the utility. Thus, our problem is also similar to the multiple secretary problem, which is to select the best m items out of the total $n > m$ items in an online fashion [10]. Instead of the ordinal criterion, Babaioff *et al.* present generalized secretary problems as a framework for online auctions which defines the objective in terms of the numerical values of items [11]. Different from these models, the selection problem studied by us involves a special assignment, i.e. interval scheduling [12]; this combination is also known as an online problem of admission control [1,3]. Given that jobs arrive online, a scheduler needs to choose whether to schedule each job to maximize the gain. An acceptance notification can either be given when the job really starts or be given once it can be feasibly scheduled. The latter is the same as the requirement of our problem, but our model permits all accepted jobs to be rescheduled. The scheduling part in our work may be relatively easy, but the online acceptance decision becomes more complex. The reason is that the decision on the current job may influence the decisions about all future jobs in our problem rather than the next few jobs in the problem of interval scheduling.

The problem in [2] is more similar to our work, but the goal is different. They use greedy algorithms, e.g. accepting any job which can be feasibly scheduled (with commitment), and analyze competitive-ratios of these algorithms. We focus on the development of acceptance strategies to maximize the profit rather than the server's utilization and provide exact solutions. Their algorithm called GREEDY can indeed be used for our problem as well and is actually very similar to our single-threshold strategy with a low value. Comparing the resulting average-case performance ratios, on average our other threshold-algorithms perform much better than the GREEDY algorithm.

Summarizing, our model's uniqueness lies in the combination of scheduling and selection, which are influenced by each other during the whole decision process. Our approach also provides a new direction of solving this kind of online decision problem and we evaluate the performance of online solutions by the average-case performance ratio instead of the worst-case competitive ratio.

6   Conclusion and Future Work

In this paper, we have introduced and studied an online decision problem which requires an agent to make acceptance decisions on sequential job offers. The objective is to maximize the utility, the sum of the payments of all accepted jobs. During the whole offering process, the agent's concern is the limited time resources and the expectation of high-payment jobs in the future.

We have presented both theoretical and heuristic solutions. In a fundamental case with unit time windows and uniform distributions, when it is necessary to use the simplest one, our theoretical single threshold strategy $T1T$ can provide the optimal value of the threshold. Our theoretical n threshold strategy TnT can generate the theoretically optimal outcomes in expectation when the number of jobs n is known and still has the best performance amongst all proposed strategies when n is unknown. From fundamental settings to complex settings, compared to the optimal offline solutions, the average-case performance ratios achieved by our online solutions are around 1.1. Overall, the strategy of three-piece piecewise linear function $PLF3$ performs very close to the theoretically optimal online solution in the fundamental case and shows the best performance in all complex settings. As it only has 6 parameters determined by the EA, we say it is a high performance solution which can be specified in a short time. Other heuristics, e.g. $H1T, H3T, PLF, PLF2$, are also very good online solutions requiring even less EA searching time. Even without sufficient training, strategy HnT also generates good results and its performance can be improved if time permits.

Through the experimental analysis, we have pointed out the impact of one key factor, i.e. the ratio between the number of slots and the number of jobs t/n, on the strategy performance. When t/n is at the middle part of $[0, 1]$, the online decision is most difficult. Although the performance of our solutions is a little lower in this part, the performance ratios between 1.09 and 1.22 illustrate the advantage of our solutions for this dynamic problem. Given various settings, in which it is difficult to find any analytical clue, our solutions show their generality, robustness and adaptivity. Although we make an assumption of unit processing time for all jobs, this work provides an approach that also applies to more generic problems involving both acceptance decisions and complex scheduling. For instance, the heuristic strategies proposed by us could be used in settings with arbitrary length jobs.

Through this work, we have learned that EAs can be used to tune the relevant parameters for settings that are hard to analyze theoretically; this thus gives a general approach, which also works for new settings (although we don't know how good it is in new settings). We answered questions such as i) how to deal with acceptance decisions and scheduling separately, ii) how to find good acceptance strategies, even if it is very hard or impossible to derive an optimal strategy (in expectation) analytically, and iii) which heuristic strategy works best (PLF3), and why (a good balance between accuracy and number of parameters).

In our future work, we would like to derive theoretically optimal solutions for general time windows in addition to our heuristic solutions. Another interesting topic is to extend the problem to a model where the processing time of jobs can vary. We may still use the approach presented in this work but need to add other key factors especially related to scheduling to achieve good results in complex environments. Analysis of competitive-ratios of our algorithms will also be included in our next work.

References

1. Goldwasser, M., Kerbikov, B.: Admission control with immediate notification. Journal of Scheduling 6(3), 269–285 (2003)
2. Garay, J., Naor, J., Yener, B., Zhao, P.: On-line admission control and packet scheduling with interleaving. In: Proc. of INFOCOM 2002, vol. 1, pp. 94–103. IEEE (2002)
3. Fung, S.P.Y.: Online Preemptive Scheduling with Immediate Decision or Notification and Penalties. In: Thai, M.T., Sahni, S. (eds.) COCOON 2010. LNCS, vol. 6196, pp. 389–398. Springer, Heidelberg (2010)
4. Ford, L., Fulkerson, D.: Maximal flow through a network. Canadian Journal of Mathematics 8(3), 399–404 (1956)
5. Bosman, P.: On empirical memory design, faster selection of bayesian factorizations and parameter-free gaussian EDAs. In: Proc. of the 11th Annual Conference on Genetic and Evolutionary Computation, pp. 389–396. ACM (2009)
6. Kuhn, H.: The Hungarian method for the assignment problem. Naval Research Logistics Quarterly 2(1-2), 83–97 (1955)
7. Buehren, M.: Algorithms for the Assignment Problem (2009),
   http://www.markusbuehren.de
8. Kalyanasundaram, B., Pruhs, K.: On-line weighted matching. In: Proc. of the Second Annual ACM-SIAM Symposium on Discrete Algorithms, p. 240. SIAM (1991)
9. Khuller Stephen, G., et al.: On-line algorithms for weighted bipartite matching and stable marriages. Theoretical Computer Science 127(2), 255–267 (1994)
10. Ajtai, M., Megiddo, N., Waarts, O.: Improved algorithms and analysis for secretary problems and generalizations. In: Proc. of the 36th Annual Symposium on Foundations of Computer Science, pp. 473–482. IEEE (1995)
11. Babaioff, M., Immorlica, N., Kempe, D., Kleinberg, R.: Online auctions and generalized secretary problems. ACM SIGecom Exchanges 7(2), 1–11 (2008)
12. Goldman, S.A., Parwatikar, J., Suri, S.: On-line Scheduling with Hard Deadlines. In: Rau-Chaplin, A., Dehne, F., Sack, J.-R., Tamassia, R. (eds.) WADS 1997. LNCS, vol. 1272, pp. 258–271. Springer, Heidelberg (1997)

Author Index